Lee Holmes discovered 'supercharged' food after she was diagnosed with an autoimmune disease in 2006. Eager to find a drug-free solution, she became a keen food and health researcher and developed a diet regime that led to her full recovery. Lee is a regular columnist for *wellbeing* magazine and a writer for Miranda Kerr's *KORA Organics* blog. She is also the woman behind the popular website www.superchargedfood.com.

SUPERCHARGED FOOD

EAT YOUR WAY TO
GOOD HEALTH

LEE HOLMES

MURDOCH BOOKS

contents

Supercharge your life

If you're looking to 'supercharge' your life with a nutritious eating plan, want to have mountains of energy and feel fantastic, then this is the book for you.

Supercharged Food offers a wealth of satisfying gluten, wheat, dairy, yeast and sugar-free recipes, so you can dine superbly on nutrient-rich and flavoursome foods whatever your dietary requirements. This book is all about keeping it real, with simple, uncomplicated and versatile recipes that will help you live a healthy lifestyle without compromising on taste.

Whether you're just starting your adventures in the kitchen or you're a food connoisseur, you'll find plenty of tips and advice about ingredients, 'superstar foods' and shopping. You'll also find ample menu options to suit any occasion, from breakfast to lunch, dinner to dessert and beyond, including yummy snacks and ideas for school lunches or seasonal soirees with friends.

And no one will ever suspect they're indulging in gluten, wheat, dairy, yeast, and sugar-free food!

My story

One winter morning in 2006 I woke to find myself barely able to get out of bed. My body was rigid and hurting and every move I made took a gigantic effort. The pain and lethargy stayed with me and even though I continued to drag myself into work, I would limp home exhausted, barely mustering the energy to flop on the couch. My stomach ached, objecting to any foods I tried to eat, raging and gurgling like a squally sea. Dinner became a non-event and all I wanted to do was curl up and sleep.

Doctors couldn't understand why I was so ill. My hair was falling out in clumps, hives covered my ulcerated body, my muscles ached and the scales barely registered 45 kg (99 lbs). Tired and depressed, self-conscious and alone, I spent the next six months in a blur, negotiating my way through a complex medical system and being passed around a parade of doctors, shuffling from one test to another with no answer on the horizon. My once fortunate life was in mayhem.

Finally a diagnosis was reached: I was suffering from a non-specific autoimmune disease and fibromyalgia. Hovering over me, doctors decided my fate — a life of immunosuppressants, steroids and anti-inflammatories, which only made me feel worse.

I knew there had to be something else I could do. Fed up with the medical system, I began to wonder whether my illness was diet related. What if I could find foods that would not irritate my condition? What if I could alter my diet, and in the process build up my immune system so I could live my old life again, free of drugs? It was worth a shot and I was determined to try.

And so my quest began. Fervently I researched, consumed, read and soaked up as much information as I could about diet and nutrition, even travelling the world to discover which nutrient-rich foods would benefit me. My learning curve was enormous. What I found opposed nearly everything I had studied in my previous food and technology classes — as if the conventional 'food pyramid' had turned itself upside down into an alternative paradigm. I discovered foods that I could use as 'medicine' to heal my body at cellular level and restore my health. I realised that for myself and many others, there is a direct correlation between what we eat and how we feel.

Changing my diet had a monumental effect on my health. I felt like I had woken from a dream. For the first time in many months I had mental clarity

The part can never be well unless the whole is well. – PLATO

and I felt alive, my high-school-nerd head spinning with ideas for new recipes, experimenting daily with a combination of different flavours and spices and unfamiliar ingredients. I was finally back in my element, cooking up a storm in the search for healthy, nutrient-rich recipes that were simple to make, yet fantastic in taste.

I devised an eating plan that would not only heal my body and provide all the nutrients I needed to get well, but offered hundreds of options for fresh, full-flavoured, easy-to-cook, beautiful foods that attracted my eye and warmed my heart. I stopped focusing on what I couldn't have, and started thinking instead about all the delicious health-promoting foods I could enjoy.

My diet has never been as exciting and satisfying as it is now. I've regained my health and vitality, and now have boundless energy and enthusiasm for life. I'm giddy with happiness to have been given the opportunity to share my insights with you, and I hope that you'll benefit as much as I have from the many delicious recipes in this book.

It's all about you

This book has been written for you, and your story. Rather than following all the recipes to the letter, please use them as a guide for developing your own personal recipes and finding the food that feeds you — whether you have chosen to eat gluten, wheat, dairy, yeast or sugar-free, or you're just looking for a way to spring clean your diet and banish fatigue.

Expanding your range of healthy food choices will become easier and allow you to plan ahead and create your own feel-good shopping list. You'll discover how to enhance your health by combining specific foods to create unique culinary delights. All of the recipes are quick and easy to make, and once you've learnt the art of stockpiling you'll be able to dive in and instantly enjoy simple recipes that will heal and nourish your body.

Pore over this book and you'll find tips on detoxing, my favourite 'top 10 superstar superfoods', and foods to avoid to maintain your long-term health and wellbeing. Say goodbye to Groundhog Day and hello to no-nonsense, mix-and-match dishes that you can jazz up to suit your dietary needs and desires. There's no reason your life needs to be compromised or lived out of a packet!

If you're looking for inspiration, the best place to start is to flick through the recipes. Find some you think you'll enjoy, then work on your own 'Supercharge your life' plan that will bring out the best in you.

✳ *Supercharged tip* Consuming a diet with a variety of wholefoods, fresh produce and ingredients as close to their natural state as possible will be less taxing on the immune system and promote healing at a cellular level.

Why 'supercharged' food?

Over the last few years I've noticed that more people are seeking healthier, more natural and allergy-friendly foods. Reasons for this range from dissatisfaction with large-scale farming methods and the industrialisation of food to concerns about the impact of chemical-laden, additive-filled and highly processed foods on our bodies, our health and our planet.

Wholefoods and gluten-free foods have become more popular due to a rise in 'modern' diseases such as autoimmune disorders, Crohn's disease, coeliac disease, irritable bowel syndrome, ulcerative colitis, candida, and food allergies and intolerances. Food has become a path to healing: it's very clear now that the food choices we make can greatly contribute to preventing disease, enhancing energy, increasing vitality and boosting the immune system.

A return to consuming unprocessed, whole and nutrient-rich foods is the realisation of a generation of people that choosing fresh, home-cooked food over commercial and industrial alternatives enhances overall health and wellbeing and helps create a foundation for optimum health. Many of us now crave food that is bursting with vitamins and minerals — food that is real and honest, without hidden salts, sugars and additives.

Real food is medicine
Great food and a healthy diet means enjoying full flavours and invigorating meals while relishing the fresh, simple and unadulterated.

The philosophy of using food as medicine is not a new one. For centuries, cultures across the world have adhered to this wisdom. It's only in the past hundred years that food manufacturing processes and preservation methods have changed. Preserving techniques that were used before then — such as smoking, canning, pickling, salting and dehydrating — were naturally-based and did not use added artificial ingredients.

After processes that can damage our foods (such as irradiation, pasteurisation and hydrogenation) were introduced, modern diseases escalated. Now the use of pesticides, herbicides and hormones in farming and the addition of artificial flavourings, colourings and preservatives in processing have changed the foods we eat. Add that to a time-poor society and you have a recipe for disaster.

Modern processed food, which guarantees longer shelf-live and is produced in high quantities, has been created to fulfil market needs. The look, packaging and taste of these products have altered our perception of food. Our palates have changed so much that many of us no longer recognise what 'real' food looks or even tastes like. Our consciousness has changed and food has become the fulfilment of an emotional need to fuel our lives in the fast lane.

Sadly, even the gluten-free market has jumped on the bandwagon, capitalising on time-poor consumers by churning out alluring gluten-free products that are often loaded with sugar or additives and unhealthy ingredients to compensate for the lack of gluten. They are expensive too — $15 for a cup and a half of sugar, a truckload of modified starches and refined cheap white rice flour. And the taste? You may as well be eating the packaging.

The truth is, we don't need a spoonful of sugar to make the medicine go down. The unnecessary

You don't have to cook fancy or complicated masterpieces — just good food from fresh ingredients. – JULIA CHILD

additives in commercially produced food are hard for our bodies to process and put extra strain on compromised immune systems. The key to my own healing has been to remove foods that make my immune system work too hard, and then optimising the chance to heal by boosting my body with nutrient-rich foods.

We tend to forget about real food until our bodies remind us otherwise. We have forgotten that nature's answer to the current problem of ailing health is in our own kitchens and pantries, and we have the power to change our lives. Food's primary purpose is nutrition — a way of providing the minerals, vitamins, enzymes, antioxidants, carbohydrates, fats and proteins needed to function optimally and to heal. Proper nutrition is the fuel that maintains, drives, detoxifies and regenerates our bodies.

Processed food is loaded with sugars, artificial sweeteners, damaging hydrogenated fats and oils, white flour, chemicals, fillers, synthetic vitamins and minerals, food additives, preservatives, heavy metals and pesticides, all of which contribute to the toxicity within our bodies and are damaging the health of our planet.

Bound in layers of plastic, aluminium foil and cardboard, all of this rubbish lands in our waste bins or drains, then ends up in landfill or our waterways, affecting the lives of our aquatic animals. As manufacturing plants have been

TOP 5 KITCHEN MEDICINE-CHEST FOODS

GINGER ROOT has been used for centuries as a medicinal aid. It helps alleviate nausea, morning sickness, motion sickness, indigestion and bloating. A daily dose of ginger extract can also help reduce the pain and inflammation of osteoarthritis.

How to use: Add to Asian dishes and soups, stir-fries and teas, and use in baking and desserts.

CABBAGE is no longer the plain Jane of vegetables. Cabbage is packed with antioxidants and cancer-fighting enzymes, helping our systems fight free radicals and clear up toxins, including potential carcinogens. The fibre in cabbage helps keeps blood sugar levels stable and regulates bowel movements. Cabbage also contains glutamine, which heals the cells that line the stomach; cabbage has been shown to treat stomach ulcers when taken in large quantities over a week.

How to use: Make cabbage rolls, an Asian slaw or kim chi, add it to soups and stir-fries, or pickle it.

CINNAMON helps control blood sugar and cholesterol. This delicious spice has an antimicrobial action and is the perfect remedy for nausea or an upset stomach. Cinnamon can also boost the performance of insulin, benefiting people with adult-onset diabetes. It is also a good source of vitamin K and iron, and a very good source of fibre, calcium and manganese.

How to use: Sprinkle on meats and add to slow-cooked stews; use in baking, desserts and teas.

TURMERIC is one of nature's most powerful healers because of its anti-inflammatory, pain-killing and liver-detoxing capabilities. Turmeric can be used as a natural antiseptic and antibacterial agent, useful in disinfecting cuts and burns.

Ingesting turmeric regularly can enhance immunity and help provide sustained energy and vitality.

How to use: Add to curries, slow-cooked casseroles, chicken dishes, vegetable dishes and homemade condiments. ·

TOMATOES are a medicinal, nutritional and edible delight, found in sunny shades of ruby-red and orange, through to purple and even black. The colour of tomatoes is due to lycopene, a strong antioxidant that has been shown to reduce the risk of cancer of the prostate and colon, bladder and lungs. Lycopene is also reported to protect white blood cells, your body's first line of defence against infection.

How to use: In salads, as a rich pasta sauce, as a salsa, on a pizza, or in a homemade relish or farm-fresh tomato sauce.

centralised, we're adding to our carbon footprint by transporting all this food to the rest of the country and beyond. That's why supporting locally grown produce is so important.

Wholefood doesn't have to be expensive if you shop in-season — local markets are glorious hunting grounds for ingredients that are fresh, alive and in-the-moment. Deciding to use food as medicine is empowering and a key step in healing, whatever your current level of health. Eating original foods direct from nature will nourish your body and strengthen your immune system, and when your immune system is strong your body will heal itself in its own time.

Think of your body as a bonfire. Good-quality, properly prepared wholegrains, lean meat and protein sources, fresh vegetables, herbs, spices and good fats are the wood that will keep the fire burning cleanly, without smoking it out with unnecessary additives. On the other hand, processed, deep-fried, sugary and artificial foods burn out quickly and do not allow the body to sustain itself. By making wise wholefood choices you can help nourish your body at a cellular level.

Using food as medicine avoids the side effects that some over-the-counter medications can bring on. Certain foods can act as anti-inflammatory agents, antidepressants, diuretics, painkillers, antibiotics, and can ward off headaches, arthritis, colds, influenza, ulcers, constipation and many other disorders. See page 11 for five of my favourites.

Top 10 superstar superfoods

The best way to eat your way to health is by including nutritional superfoods in your daily diet. It's so easy to add nutrient-rich, flavoursome smart-picks to your menus and create delicious feasts that not only taste amazing, but will also bring long-term health benefits.

Nutrients in foods are synergistic — working together to benefit your entire body. Many of these superstar superfoods contain phytonutrients that promote good health due to their antioxidant and anti-inflammatory properties.

To really boost your immunity, try incorporating the following foods into your meals.

ONIONS contain a high concentration of quercetin, an antioxidant that helps protect and strengthen damaged cells. Onions are great for raising 'good' cholesterol levels, lowering high blood pressure and helping to thin the blood, warding off blood clots.
How to use: In stir-fries, scrambled eggs, baked whole with roasts, French onion soup, in stews, casseroles and pasta sauces, and added to savoury muffins.

GARLIC increases immune function by promoting the growth of white blood cells — the body's natural germ fighters. Garlic has been proven to slow the growth of harmful bacteria, yeasts and fungi. Fresh garlic is always the best choice and is a good alternative to antibiotics. Both fresh and dried garlic have been shown to lower harmful LDL cholesterol and high blood pressure. I take two crushed cloves a day with water to keep bugs out of my system and avoid picking up flus or viruses.
How to use: Fried with omelettes, crushed in garlic mash, roasted with vegetables, lamb, chicken or pork, in stir-fries and on garlic bread.

BROCCOLI is rich in magnesium and vitamin C, which is known to help fight infections and viruses and is considered to be one of the most powerful immunity boosters available. Vitamin C also promotes the production of interferon, an antibody that blocks viruses and infections from getting deep into cells.
How to use: Add to stir-fries, salads, casseroles, pasta dishes and soups, or lightly steam and serve as a side dish.

QUINOA is perfect as a fast and filling nutritional breakfast — just add almond milk for an added boost of protein. Not strictly a grain, quinoa (pronounced keen-wah) is derived from the seed of a plant related to spinach and is a true superfood. It is a complete protein food, which means it contains all the essential amino acids your body needs to

Supercharged tip Chlorophyll is a blood enricher with special nutrients that build iron and raise haemoglobin count, improving circulation and giving you extra energy. It also cleanses and improves the health of the intestines, uterus and lungs. Some people also use it as a natural breath freshener and body deodoriser.

build muscle and repair itself. As well as being high in protein, with few carbohydrates and a dose of healthy fats, quinoa contains an amino acid called lysine, in addition to vitamin B6, thiamine, niacin, potassium, riboflavin, copper, zinc, magnesium and folate.
How to use: In porridge, salads and soups, and as a side dish.

KALE is a fibre-rich, dark-green leafy vegetable that looks similar to spinach and is jam-packed with essential vitamins and minerals. The vitamin A and C in kale is fantastic for your skin and can slow down premature ageing. It also contains lutein, a nutrient that is beneficial for your body and complexion, and also brightens the whites of your eyes. One serving of cooked kale provides more than half the recommended daily allowance of vitamin C.
How to use: Add to stir-fries or hearty vegetable soups, or crisp it in the oven with extra virgin olive oil and sea salt as a nutritious snack.

WILD SALMON is a great source of protein and contains minerals such as iodine, potassium and zinc. It also contains omega-3 fats — the ultimate anti-ageing nutrient and a major component of brain and nerve tissues. Omega-3 fats are also beneficial for good eyesight. Wild salmon contains loads of vitamin D and selenium for healthy hair, skin, nails and bones. For optimum health benefits, consume salmon at least three times a week.
How to use: On sandwiches, for breakfast with poached eggs, in soups and pasta dishes, or cook up some salmon fillets.

NUTS are not only yummy, but also contain healthy oils, fibre, vitamins, minerals, potent phytochemicals and the amino acid arginine. Walnuts are one of the best plant sources of protein, and all nuts are beneficial for heart health — eating a handful of nuts five times a week reduces your risk of coronary heart disease. Nuts are rich in fibre, B vitamins, magnesium and antioxidants such as vitamin E. If you are concerned about mould and mycotoxins in nuts, soak them in water and sea salt overnight and then dry in the oven for a yummy crispy snack.
How to use: As a snack, nut milks, crunchy toppings for sweet and savoury dishes, and nut flours for baking.

SPINACH is bursting with delicious health benefits. It contains a cross-section of phytonutrients and antioxidants, including vitamins K, C and E, beta-carotene, coenzyme Q10, folate, iron and the carotenoids lutein and zeaxanthin.
How to use: In stir-fries, soups and pasta sauces, for breakfast with poached eggs, and as Spinach Toast (page 170).

SARDINES are high in omega-3 fatty acids, contain almost no mercury (unlike large fish), and are loaded with minerals such as calcium, iron, magnesium, phosphorus, potassium, zinc, copper and manganese, and are rich in vitamin B. Not a sardine fan? Try flax seeds, walnuts or chia seeds for an omega-3 blast.
How to use: Mix in a salad, serve on Spinach Toast (page 170) or buckwheat toast, serve with eggs, or use as a spread combined with mustard and apple cider vinegar.

EGGS have had a chequered past, but it has now been proven that eating eggs in moderation will not give you high cholesterol, as was originally reported. In fact, eggs have stellar stats, with high-quality proteins, essential minerals and vitamins, including vitamin B12 and folate. An egg is a compact package of nutrition that provides every vitamin except vitamin C. Eggs are also a rich source of vitamin K — one egg contains one-third of the daily recommended amount for women. I usually have about two or three servings per week.

How to use: Poached, scrambled, baked, in frittatas, omelettes, baked goods and sauces. For a quick on-the-go snack, hard-boil a batch of eggs.

For more information on superfoods, visit the website www.superchargedfood.com

The skinny on good fats

Many of us think that all fats are bad for us, raising cholesterol and causing weight gain and heart disease. In fact, natural fats and oils are vital for optimal health and immune function. The best oils to consume are cold-pressed extra virgin olive oil, fish oils and some nut and seed oils, as well as coconut oil and organic butter in moderation.

Good fats and oils provide energy and increase your body's ability to absorb nutrients such as vitamins A, D, E and K from food. Good fats and oils also act as powerful antioxidants that help rebuild cell membranes. They help the body to eliminate heavy metals such as aluminium, mercury, nickel and lead by increasing the production of bile in the liver. Heavy metals can otherwise accumulate in the body and cause health issues for many people.

The most damaging fats and oils are man-made hydrogenated fats (trans fats) and vegetable oils. These fats are difficult for the body to process due to the hydrogenation processes they have undergone and they affect the structure of cells and depress the immune system. Steer clear of canola (from rapeseed), safflower, sunflower, soya bean and corn oils. Many products such as margarine,

salad dressings, mayonnaise and cooking and baking oils contain these oils, which are often blended together, so it's good to start checking food labels. For example, if you buy tuna in olive oil, you may find that it has been blended with sunflower oil.

Swap the bad fats for the following good oils, which will keep you heart-healthy and in tip-top shape.

Olive oil

Olive oil is a natural juice that is pressed out of olives and retains the fruit's taste, aroma and vitamins. Olive oil contains a high level of monounsaturated fatty acids and antioxidants, which help protect against heart disease by controlling harmful LDL cholesterol and raising beneficial HDL cholesterol levels. The best olive oil is cold-pressed extra virgin olive oil, which contains more nutrients as it comes from the first pressing of the olives. Buy olive oil in dark bottles, to protect the oil against damage from sunlight.

Fish oils (essential fatty acids)

Omega-3 and omega-6 fatty acids are essential to health. Many modern diets contain omega-6, but not enough omega-3 fats. The best source of omega-3 is fish, which is high in two fatty acids crucial to human health: eicosapentaenoic acid (EPA) and docosahexaenoic acid (DHA). These two fatty acids can help prevent heart disease, cancer and many other diseases. Eating fish at least three times a week will boost your omega-3 intake. Meat and eggs are also good sources of essential fatty acids.

Seed and nut oils

Macadamia, grape seed, flax seed, walnut and sesame oils are all good for us, but should be consumed in moderate amounts. Sesame oil is a tasty choice for stir-fries as it contains unique antioxidants that aren't destroyed by heat. A powerful antioxidant, grape seed oil is easily digested and contains high-density lipoprotein, which helps reduce blood cholesterol. Its consistency and neutral taste make it a useful butter substitute for baking, salad dressings,

Supercharged tip If a product sells itself as being 'low fat' or 'no fat', it's most likely that the fat has been replaced with sugar, refined flour, preservatives or additives.

sautéing and frying. Flax seed oil has been reported to improve blood sugar levels, promote healthy hair and skin, and ward off arthritis due to its high content of omega-3 fatty acids. Use flax seed and walnut oil uncooked in salad dressings and spreads, and keep them in the fridge to minimise rancidity. Macadamia nut oil contains heart-friendly fatty acids and can be used for cooking omelettes, pancakes and in baking.

Coconut oil

Not all saturated fats are bad for you. Research has shown that coconut oil is a healthy saturated fat that supports immune system function. Coconut oil contains lauric acid, a proven antiviral, antibacterial and antifungal agent. Coconut oil is easily digested and helps the body absorb nutrients and eliminate toxins. Unrefined cold-pressed or expeller-pressed coconut oil is the best; it's also a safe oil to use for cooking as it has a high burning point.

Organic butter

Butter isn't dairy free, but some people who are lactose intolerant and have casein problems tolerate it well. If butter is a problem for you, stick to extra virgin olive oil, grape seed oil, coconut oil or, in some cases, ghee. Although it contains saturated fat, organic butter is an important dietary fat as it contains minerals such as manganese, zinc, chromium and iodine, as well as vitamins A (retinol), D, K and E and many other nutrients. Butter is also rich in selenium, a trace mineral with antioxidant properties.

Detoxers & natural cleansers

Our body is exposed to toxins and harmful chemicals every day. These come from the food we eat, the household and beauty products we use and even our water supply. Many of our fruits and vegetables are loaded with chemicals — sprayed with anti-ripening agents, fertilisers, herbicides and pesticides.

When we ingest these substances, a portion is broken down and eliminated from our bodies, but some remains and becomes lodged in our cells and tissues, which can result in toxic overload in the liver. Cleansing the body helps remove stored toxins.

Detox methods include ingesting herbal supplements, exercising, colonic irrigation and fasting. Some of these processes can be radical, particularly if you are unwell and have a weakened immune system.

If you're feeling clogged up, the best way to detox your body is to eat a nutrient-rich diet, along with the Supercharged Shake (page 36). A beneficial detox diet consists of eating healthy protein sources from meat, eggs and fish, along with good fats such as cold-pressed extra virgin olive oil, extra virgin coconut oil and fish oils, which contain omega-3 essential fatty acids. These good fats help eliminate toxins and heavy metals from your body and help you absorb nutrients from food, enabling the healing process. Sea salt also helps draw nutrients from food. Eating a protein source or lacto-fermented foods such as kim chi (Korean pickled cabbage) or sauerkraut increases stomach acid, which stimulates the gall bladder, helping the digestive process. Your detoxification will increase as your digestion improves.

There are bucket loads of other foods that feed the skin. If you're looking for a glowing complexion, bright eyes and shiny hair, eat foods rich in lecithin, essential fatty acids and antioxidants, such as eggs, organ meats, fresh dark-green leafy vegetables, tomatoes and berries of all kinds, and ensure you get a balance of omega-3, 6 and 9 oils.

Detoxing need not cost the earth or involve fancy-schmancy spas or invasive procedures that leave you feeling wiped out. Try these cost-effective ways to naturally detoxi your body, enhance your health and save your bank balance at the same time.

Natural lemon detox

Lemons are a fantastic detoxer and have amazing digestive qualities. A daily glass of lemon juice in water is not only a good detoxer, but also alleviates symptoms of indigestion, stomach pain and bloating. Drinking lemon juice helps the bowels eliminate waste more efficiently and controls constipation and diarrhoea. Lemons also help the body draw the energy from the nutrients in our food. Lemons are high in nutrients and bioflavonoids and are an excellent source of vitamin B6, iron and potassium, dietary fibre and vitamin C. They also contain calcium, copper, folic

 Supercharged tip If you plan to lace up your sneakers, stir up something tasty and refreshing before exercise. My secret-weapon lemon electrolyte drink will keep your body functioning well and help you stay hydrated. Simply fill your water bottle with purified water, add a teaspoon of sea salt and the juice of half a lemon, drink it, and prepare to pump it up.

acid, magnesium, manganese, phosphorus and zinc. I often use lemon juice and garlic as an antibacterial; it is also particularly effective as an antiseptic gargle for sore throats or mouth ulcers.

For your daily natural lemon detox, follow these steps:

- Squeeze the juice of half a lemon into a glass.
- Pour in freshly boiled warm filtered water.
- Add stevia (see page 20) to taste.
- Drink once a day, preferably upon rising or before a meal.

Detox baths

I love to linger in a soothing epsom salts bath after a hectic day working and running around after the family. It's important to take time out and devote at least 20 minutes each day to complete relaxation. The magnesium sulphate in an epsom salts bath is absorbed through the skin, eliminating toxins from the body. It also calms the nervous system, reduces swelling, relaxes muscles and relieves aches and pains. Epsom salts are a natural emollient and exfoliator, so use them instead of expensive exfoliants for smooth, glowing skin.

To prepare an epsom salts bath, add two standard cups of salts to a warm bath while the water is running. Soak your body for 15–20 minutes — the stress will float right away. Sip on a herbal tea at the same time for the ultimate relaxation.

Dry skin brushing

Your skin is your body's largest and most important organ of elimination, responsible for one-quarter of your body's detoxification. Dry skin brushing has been used for thousands of years as a natural way of detoxing the body. This gentle practice has internal as well as external benefits. It stimulates the lymphatic system, liver and adrenal glands, helping these organs clear out toxins while giving the body a gentle internal massage. It also improves liver and adrenal gland function, strengthens the immune system, stimulates circulation and helps prevent dry skin. The exfoliating effect of dry skin brushing removes dead skin layers and stimulates skin renewal. It also helps remove cellulite and tightens the skin to help prevent premature ageing.

How to do dry skin brushing

Use a bath brush with natural bristles, as synthetic bristles can irritate the skin. Use the brush only for this purpose and keep it dry to retain the bristles. A long-handled brush is good for getting to those hard-to-reach places. Wash the brush with soap and water every few weeks to keep it clean. When brushing, make sure your skin is completely dry. The brush should pass once over every part of the body, except the face. Use long, gentle, but firm strokes. Begin with your feet and continue brushing upwards, and take extra care on your chest. The best time to brush your skin is in the morning before your shower or bath.

Salt water flushes

A salt water flush is one of the easiest, cheapest and quickest ways to clean your colon at home. Salt water flushes cleanse your stomach and small intestine, flushing out toxins and bacteria from your digestive tract. There are many expensive laxatives, enemas and cleansing products that temporarily alleviate symptoms, but a salt water flush works just as well and is a much gentler alternative.

The best time to do a salt water flush is first thing in the morning, before breakfast. I guarantee you will feel lighter and more energised.

How to do a salt water flush

- Fill a drinking container with 1 litre (35 fl oz/4 cups) of warm filtered water.
- Add 1 heaped tablespoon of ocean sea salt and the juice of half a lemon.
- Sprinkle in stevia powder (see page 20) if you would like to sweeten the taste.
- Drink slowly and await the results.
- Don't make any plans for the next 20 minutes and make sure you are close to a bathroom!

Foods to avoid

Over time, eating the wrong foods can adversely affect our health. Some foods can be difficult to digest, contain ingredients that stress our bodies, cause allergic reactions or slowly poison us.

Digestion is hard work for our bodies, but it is essential for releasing energy from the food we consume. Our bodies break proteins down into amino acids, carbohydrates into simple sugars, and fats into fatty acids, and these are then absorbed into our digestive system and carried into the blood and into our cells. At the cellular level, the energy from our food then fuels the body.

For these processes to occur we need an abundance of reserve energy from our food. That's why we should eat foods that are easy to digest, yet nutrient-rich, and limit our intake of processed and artificial foods.

Foods that are high in saturated fats, sugars and refined flours — such as pizza, fast food, ice cream and sugary desserts — take a lot of energy to digest, making us feel tired and bloated. Any doctor will tell you that the common modern diet, full of sugar, salt and the wrong kinds of fat, has a negative effect on our bodies in the long term.

When you first go on a gluten, wheat, dairy, yeast and sugar-free diet, you may actually feel worse before you get better; this is good news because your body is getting rid of stored toxins. A good way to navigate through this period is to be kind to yourself, get as much rest as possible, and drink plenty of water with lemon juice, as vitamin C is a powerful antioxidant that helps flush toxins from the body.

After a few weeks of experimenting with the recipes in this book, you'll feel energised, alive and ready for anything. Your tastebuds will also be transformed and you'll no longer crave the foods you've given up. In fact, if you do eat them you'll be surprised at how bad they actually taste! You'll develop a yearning for real food — food that is genuine, healthy and simply delicious.

If you are immunocompromised or suffer from digestive problems, your health may benefit considerably by avoiding the following common foods:

WHEAT, COW'S MILK AND SOY PRODUCTS are poor choices for people with low-functioning immune systems. Wheat products contain glue in the form of gluten, and milk contains casein and lactose. These substances are incredibly difficult for many people to digest and can contribute to a wide range of digestive disorders.

The glue in wheat products can in some cases cause holes in the lining of the intestines, leading to poor nutrient absorption, leaky gut syndrome and fibromyalgia. Toxins can then pass through the damaged intestinal wall, causing rapid firing of neurons in the brain — the reason for 'brain fog', depression and anxiety. Studies have shown that 'modern' diseases such as Crohn's disease, coeliac disease, irritable bowel syndrome, candida and food allergies are caused by vitamin and mineral deficiencies resulting from poor digestion or nutrient absorption.

People who have damaged intestinal walls may need to drink nutrient-rich shakes and eat soups and easily absorbed foods to give their bodies a chance to heal.

Certain inhibitors in soy products block protein and nutrient absorption, which can also cause abdominal distress in some people. Soy products include soya beans, soy protein, soybean oil, soy lecithin and soy derivatives. Watch out for soy lecithin, an emulsifier that's added to many of our processed foods. It is also found in certain organic and gluten-free foods, so check the label to ensure it's not genetically modified. Soybean oil is another additive that is generally derived from genetically modified soya beans, and is common in foods such as mayonnaise and salad dressings, and even baked goods such as breads and cakes.

If you do like soy, the best way to consume it is in its whole, organic and fermented state, eating products such as miso, tempeh and tamari in moderation.

PROCESSED FOODS and those containing artificial ingredients are best avoided. The processing component removes vitamins and minerals from foods, diminishing their nutritional value. After food has been processed, artificial ingredients and additives are then added to enhance its flavour, taste and shelf-life. After long-term consumption these foods and additives begin to wreak havoc on the immune system.

Unfortunately, children's foods contain many additives and colourants that children can react badly to. Evidence has shown that these have contributed to the rise in children in conditions such as ADHD, asthma, diabetes, food allergies and digestive disorders, as well as obesity and hyperactivity.

SUGAR consumption has been associated with heart disease, autoimmune diseases, diabetes, irritable bowel disease, chronic fatigue, candida and many pain-related conditions. Sugar can inhibit the absorption of vitamin C into white blood cells, causing reduced immunity. Sugar in all forms should be avoided, or limited as much as possible. This includes white and brown sugar, too much fruit, and sugar substitutes. Countless low-fat meals have artificial sugars added, and there is evidence to suggest that these artificial sugars also have adverse side effects.

TABLE SALT should be replaced with the much healthier sea salt. Many fast foods are jam-packed with table salt, as are tinned and packaged foods. Table salt usually contains anti-caking agents and additives, and has gone through several chemical processes before it hits the table; consuming too much table salt can also contribute to high blood pressure and heart disease. Sea salt contains all the elements of the ocean and minerals that help draw essential nutrients from food. It has also been reported to lower blood pressure and assist with

water retention. I like to use Celtic sea salt in my recipes: as well as providing valuable minerals, it has a wonderful taste.

CAFFEINE is found in many drinks and foodstuffs, the most common being coffee, black tea, cola drinks, cocoa and chocolate. It is also an ingredient in a number of over-the-counter medicines. Caffeine belongs to a class of chemicals called methylxanthines, which act as a central nervous system stimulant — increasing alertness, speeding up metabolism, stimulating the cardiovascular system, increasing the heart and respiratory rates, and elevating blood pressure. Caffeine is addictive, so people find they need increasingly larger amounts to keep their energy up. Caffeine also stimulates the release of stress hormones from the adrenal glands; over time, adrenal exhaustion can lead to persistent fatigue. Caffeine can also aggravate anxiety and contributes to the loss of potassium, zinc, magnesium and vitamins B and C from the body. You don't have to give up coffee altogether, but limiting it to one or two cups a day is a good option — or better still, drink decaffeinated Swiss water-processed coffee or dandelion tea.

MAN-MADE FATS such as some vegetable oils and especially trans fats (which are hydrogenated liquid oils) are not a wise choice. Trans fats increase the risk of heart disease and are mostly found in commercially packaged foods and fried fast foods. They can also be found in commercial popcorn, vegetable shortening and hard stick margarine. The best fats to stick to are cold-pressed extra virgin olive oil, seed and nut oils, and moderate amounts of coconut oil (and raw butter if you can tolerate it).

If you are unsure about what to buy, try to choose foods that are as close to nature as possible. Eating more gluten-free grains like quinoa and buckwheat, low-fructose fresh fruits, a multitude of brightly coloured vegetables, moderate amounts of protein and limiting man-made fats will provide balanced nutrition for the body and mind. In a nutshell, say yes to real produce — enjoy all kinds of garden-fresh seasonal vegies, organic meat, chicken eggs and unfarmed fish for those spiffy omega-3 oils. When I switched to a wholefoods diet I noticed the benefits almost immediately.

Numbers, additives and preservatives

We are confronted daily with a plethora of additives in our food, many of them cleverly disguised. Food additives can contribute to a wide array of health issues, although reactions can vary from person to person. If a product contains preservatives, chemicals, fillers, artificial flavours or artificial colours, the best place to leave it is on the shelf. By educating ourselves and becoming adept at reading food labels, we can avoid buying these products and create a new market need for whole, fresh and pure foods. Copy out the following lists and take them to the supermarket with you next time you go shopping.

Artificial colours

Artificial colours and food dyes are found in soft drinks, fruit juices, salad dressings, hotdogs, cereals, sweets and baked goods. They are prevalent in many children's products and can cause behavioural problems, learning delay, hives, rashes and migraines. Some of them are 102, 103, 104, 110, 120, 122–129, 131, 132, 133, 140, 142, 143, 150, 151, 155, 160b (annatto), 162, 164.

Preservatives

The numbers are stacking up against food preservatives. New studies have shown that approximately one in a hundred people are sensitive to sulphites in food. Common symptoms include rashes, breathing difficulties and

30 SUGARS UNCOVERED

Agave	High-fructose corn syrup	Malt	Raw (demerara) sugar
Brown sugar		Maltodextrin	Refined sugar
Cane sugar	High-maltose corn syrup	Maltose	Rice syrup
Corn syrup		Maple syrup	Sucrose
Fructose	Honey	Molasses	Table sugar
Glactose	Icing (confectioners') sugar	Muscovado sugar	Treacle
Granulated sugar		Palm sugar (jaggery)	Turbinado sugar
Grape sugar	Invert sugar	Panocha	White sugar
	Lactose		

headaches. Wine and dried fruit are the most common foods that contain sulphites.

    Sorbates 200–203

    Benzoates 210–213

    Sulphites 220–228

    Nitrates, nitrites 249–252

    Food acids 260–264, 270

    Propionates 280–283

Antioxidant additives

Gallates 310–312; TBHQ, BHA, BHT 319–321, butylated hydroxyanisole (BHA) and butylated hydrozytoluene (BHT) are preservatives that retain a food's colour and flavour and stop it going off. They can cause neurological disturbances and alter behaviour. They are found mainly in vegetable oils, cereals, potato chips, sweets and chewing gum.

Vegetable gums and thickeners

Carrageenan 407

Guar gum 412

Methylcellulose 461, 464, 465, 466

Xanthan gum 415

Flavour enhancers

Glutamates, MSG 620–625

Disodium guanylate 627

Disodium inosinate 631

Ribonucleotides 635

Hydrolysed vegetable protein (HVP)

The lowdown on labels

It's easy to decode food labels for any numbers, additives or preservatives using the additive list. In general, numbers 100–180 are colours, numbers 200–290 are preservatives, numbers 300–320 are antioxidants, and numbers 322–494 are emulsifiers. Some additives are harmless, so it's good to know the difference — for more information, pick up an additive pocket guide. MSG (621) is a flavour enhancer that should be avoided; sometimes it's disguised on labels as hydrolysed vegetable protein. Adverse reactions to MSG can include nausea, migraine, anxiety, sleeplessness, skin rashes and abdominal pain.

The best way to read a food label is from the ingredients list, not the nutritional information panel, which details the percentage of fibre, carbohydrates, fat and so on that the product contains. Examining the ingredients list will help you identify whether the food is from nature or made in a laboratory. A food labelled 'natural' may still include processed ingredients, so don't be fooled by marketing buzz words, which are often misleading.

Endorsements on the packaging from companies and foundations only focus on the food's overall nutrition and not the ingredients, so even if something has a tick of approval it can still contain extremely unhealthy ingredients.

Rule out any food that contains artificial sweeteners. When a product is labelled 'sugar free', it almost certainly contains one form of artificial sweetener or another. I once believed that artificial sugars were 'better' for me than sugar as they were lower in calories, so I was sprinkling them into my tea and using them in desserts. I was horrified to learn that artificial sweeteners can cause a horror movie of side effects, such as palpitations, skin rashes, migraines, stomach ache, seizures — and in some people, hallucinations!

Here is a list of sneaky artificial sweeteners or, as I like to call them, naughty number nines.

Artificial sweeteners

950 Acesulfame potassium

951 Aspartame (Nutrasweet, Equal)

952 Sodium cyclamate

952 Cyclamic acid

952 Calcium cyclamate

953 Isomalt (humectant)

954 Sodium saccharin

954 Saccharin

954 Calcium saccharin

955 Sucralose

956 Alitame

957 Thaumatin

965 Maltitol and maltitol syrup (humectant, stabiliser)

966 Lactitol (humectant)

967 Xylitol (humectant, stabiliser)

Getting started

Getting started may be a challenge, but once you become familiar with the ingredients and recipes in this book, eating well will become second nature. Don't worry if you haven't cooked with whole, unprocessed foods before. I'm going to give you some fantastic meal ideas, a shopping list and menu choices so you can plan ahead. The trick is to start simply, follow the recipes and then, once you're comfortable, branch out and enjoy your own creations. Good-quality ingredients are worth investing in, such as extra virgin olive oil and unfiltered apple cider vinegar.

To start, look through the recipes and see what you like. You can change the recipes depending on what ingredients you prefer to use. For example, if you'd rather use agave than stevia, you can swap these ingredients and experiment with taste. (But remember, agave is still a sugar.) Soon you'll be enjoying simple slow-cooked Greek lamb, perky Thai-style dishes, salads with crunch and flavoursome Indian curries, without compromising taste for well being.

Next, look through the weekly menu planner and compile a menu that suits your needs. Over time this list will evolve. Eventually you can start devising your own appetising meals using the shopping list as a guide, or adding new ingredients based on the whole food principles.

Once you've organised your shopping list, you can set aside a day for 'batch cooking' — perhaps on a Sunday if you work full-time or don't have the time to cook every day. If you're a busy mum, ask your partner or a friend to look after the children for a few hours, or ask the kids to help out in the kitchen. You could even invite some friends over and make a day of it.

For a step-by-step guide on how to get started, read on.

Step 1

Look through the recipes and choose your favourites, making sure you include a variety of foods. If you have a sweet tooth, you'll still be able to enjoy delicious desserts and baked goods minus the sugar.

Step 2

Plan a weekly menu, using the sample weekly menu as a guide. I have a blackboard in my kitchen on which I write down my meals for the week. I also put my shopping list on it.

Clear highly processed foods or products that contain additives, preservatives or food enhancers from your kitchen cupboards. There is more about this on the following pages. Remember, eating real food — not numbers — is the key to better health.

Step 3

Go shopping. If you're time poor, you can order your weekly shopping online from an organic grocer that home-delivers. Visit a major supermarket for household staples — they have own-brand organic products at affordable prices. Buy organic if it's within your budget, but if the organaholic lifestyle is out of reach, simply wash the fruit and vegetables you buy in lemon and vinegar to remove pesticides and fertilisers. (You can do this with a scrubbing brush in the sink.) Organic food is not as expensive as it used to be and it is also more readily available. If you can only afford a few organic products, buy organic eggs and vegetables. Incidentally, if you do buy organic meat, you can make it go a long way by using the offcuts to make stock.

Buying organic meat from supermarkets at night can save you money as it is discounted by up to 50% if it's near its use-by date. I usually go on a Wednesday or Thursday evening. The best place to buy fresh fruit and vegetables is at your local farmers' market, any organic market or your local greengrocer. Eating from farmers' markets supports local farmers, too. To reduce cost, choose recipes that make the most of in-season fruit and vegetables.

You can also grow your own herbs, so you always have fresh herbs at your fingertips. If you live in an apartment you can use a windowsill. I have a thriving herb garden on my patio and whenever I'm cooking I reach out and grab a fistful. Any herbs that I don't use I dehydrate for the winter months. Commercially dried herbs are often irradiated, so growing your own and dehydrating the excess is a healthier option.

Household cleaning products can also be inexpensive if you use natural products such as white vinegar and bicarbonate of soda (baking soda).

Step 4
Batch cooking is a great way to make staple items such as breads, sauces and soups to enjoy during the week. Batch cooking makes home management easier, saves time and money and means you'll be less tempted to buy expensive convenience foods.

The key to batch cooking is to make large amounts that can be frozen and used when you have no time to prepare meals. Stews, casseroles, soups, curries and shepherd's pie are great stockpile meals. Double the quantities in the recipes and you will have enough to last a fortnight or more. Remember to label and date each batch.

Step 5
Now it's time to prepare the yummy recipes. Once you start enjoying wonderful whole food meals, you'll feel energised and excited about what you can create. Cooking will become fun, with the benefit of knowing you are feeding and healing your body with wholesome, nutrient-rich foods. Escaping to the kitchen is also an ideal way to unwind and be creative, and sharing wonderful home-cooked meals is a great way to reconnect with the family. In the beginning my family wasn't keen on eating anything different; now I get complaints when I don't cook the recipes.

Step 6
After using the recipes for a few weeks and eliminating processed food, grains, dairy and sugar from your diet, your body will start to detoxify. The next step is to rebuild your immune system. You can do this by drinking a daily nutritional shake or Green Renewal Juice (see page 32) using any mixture of spinach, kale, mint, parsley, cucumber, lettuce, celery and ginger, which makes the body less acidic and aids detoxification. The shakes are super convenient, perfect for breakfast and provide nutrients to build healthy cells and support a strong immune system.

You can also buy prepared green shakes and powders, but it's better to make your own so you know exactly what's in it. Nutritional shakes from health food stores or pharmacies often contain synthetic ingredients, fillers and artificial sugars that undo your new diet's beneficial work. If you have a touchy digestive system and malabsorption problems, taking pills and synthetic nutraceuticals will be a waste of time and money.

Food is our nourishment and a powerful vehicle for transformation, so the best place to start is to monitor the way you feel inside after eating. By listening to your body's signals, making changes and keeping things simple you will know what works for you. Remember, you are your body's best teacher.

Pantry makeover
Giving your pantry a dietary makeover is a key element to improving nutrition and promoting healthy eating. If you're super busy, it's important to have ingredients for meals at your fingertips so you're not tempted to snack on junk, overeat, or not eat at all.

There's another big benefit to possessing a well-organised pantry. No one wants to lift the lid on a half-eaten pudding from two Christmases ago, find foamy, shrivelled-up potatoes with tentacles, spices with no flavour, or be horrified to discover that brown bugs have been partying up a storm in

SUPERCHARGED SHOPPING LIST (CHOOSE FROM THE FOLLOWING)

Vegetables

Artichoke
Asparagus
Avocado
Bok choy
Broccoli
Brussels sprouts
Cabbage
Capsicum (pepper)
Cauliflower
Celery
Cucumber
Daikon
Eggplant (aubergine)
Fennel
Garlic
Green beans
Kale
Leek
Lettuce
Okra
Olives
Onions
Pumpkin (winter squash)
Radish
Rocket (arugula)
Shallots
Snow peas (mangetout)
Spring onions (scallions)
Swede (rutabaga)
Yellow baby (pattypan) squash
Sea vegetables
Spinach
Sprouts
Tomatoes
Turnip
Watercress
Zucchini (courgette)

Meats & protein

Beef
Lamb
Pork
Bacon/ham (nitrate and sugar free)
Organ meats
Veal
Chicken
Duck
Turkey
Quail
Eggs

Seafood

Fresh fish
Anchovies
Prawns (shrimp)
Squid
Tuna
Salmon (wild caught)
Sardines
Scallops
Shellfish
Oysters

Fats & oils

Organic butter (if tolerated)
Ghee
Extra virgin olive oil (cold pressed)
Coconut oil (extra virgin)
Seed oils (grapeseed, flax seed, sesame)
Nut oils (macadamia, walnut)

Nuts, seeds and nut butters

Hazelnut
Brazil
Macadamia
Pecan
Walnut
Almond
Pepitas (pumpkin seeds)
Flax seeds
Sesame seeds
Tahini

Flours & Baking

Buckwheat
Quinoa
Millet
Amaranth
Buckwheat flour
Coconut flour
Almond meal
Brown rice flour
Tapioca flour
Bicarbonate of soda (baking soda)
Baking powder (gluten-free)
Coconut flakes

Beverages

Decaffeinated coffee/tea
Herbal teas/tisanes
Dandelion tea
Mineral/soda water (club soda)
Coconut water

Herbs & spices

Basil
Rosemary
Oregano
Coriander (cilantro)
Parsley
Sage
Thyme
Tarragon
Chives
Ginger
Nutmeg
Cinnamon
Whole cloves
Vanilla beans

Condiments/sauces

Mustard powder
Celtic sea salt
Whole peppercorns
Wheat-free tamari
Stevia liquid
Stevia powder
Apple cider vinegar
Nutritional yeast flakes
Coconut milk

Fruits (low in fructose)

Lemons
Limes
Berries
All other fruits in moderation

Supplements

Calcium
Magnesium
Probiotics
Cod liver oil
Fish oil
Vitamins B, C, D and E

Healthy home

Epsom salts
White vinegar
Eucalyptus oil
Lemon juice
Tea tree oil

✳ *Supercharged tip* Having food properly organised and safely contained in the fridge will stop your leftovers becoming last week's science experiments. Allow for good air circulation by not overfilling the fridge. Store leftovers in airtight containers to enhance longevity, eliminate wastage and not affect other foods.

all those dried goods. If you do have an invitation to an evil weevil party, you know it's time to reclaim your pantry and stock it with new, healthy ingredients.

Plan to begin Project-New-Pantry on a day where you can devote at least an hour to the task. Arm yourself with the right tools for the job and if you can rope in a business partner, all the better. Have on hand a couple of heavy-duty garbage bags or cardboard boxes for the food you're throwing or giving away, a pair of rubber gloves to protect your hands, a dustpan and brush, a cleaning cloth and white vinegar for wiping out the cupboards. You'll also need the list of additives from earlier in this chapter once it's time to scour the food labels for those nasty added ingredients.

For the ultimate pantry purge, follow this guide.

Separate the wheat from the chaff
Start in the pantry. Remove the items from the first shelf and place them on your kitchen bench or table. Check the use-by dates and place out-of-date food in one bag to be thrown away, and less healthy food in another bag to give to a local charity that accepts food donations.

If you haven't been a label reader in the past, a good rule of thumb is that foods with more than 10 ingredients are listed are unlikely to be healthy options. Check the fine print on labels for hidden ingredients. Unfortunately, not all ingredients are always declared on labels if they are present in only tiny amounts. Just do the best you can. If you're on a strict elimination diet, you can call or email a product's manufacturer to obtain a full ingredient list.

Your breakfast cereal probably contains added colouring if it changes the colour of the milk that you add. A product might also be labelled as being able to reduce cholesterol, but if it contains unnatural ingredients or chemicals, it still won't be good for you. If you look at the label on commercially made soups, you'll probably find any number of the following ingredients listed: wheat flour, soybean oil, salt, modified cornstarch, soy protein concentrate, monosodium glutamate, whey powder, yeast extract, maltodextrin, disodium phosphate, food acid, vegetable gum and flavourings and colourings. Many of these ingredients can wreak havoc on your immune system and inhibit natural healing and should be avoided. Read through the numbers, additives and preservatives list again so you know what you're looking for when shopping.

One day you're in, the next you're out
Throw out the most obvious health-sabotaging foods such as cake mixes, deep-fried foods, chips, sugar-laden cereals, biscuits, cakes, pastries, crackers, vegetable oil, hydrogenated oils, margarine and foods containing bad fats.

Once you start looking you'll notice that sugar is added to countless products: canned foods, baked goods, desserts, salad dressings, sauces, meat products, breads, cereals and soft drinks, and is disguised under many names, depending on how it's been processed. If you want to shelve sugar, the list on page 21 will help you identify its many aliases. If you're following a sugar-free diet, remember that ingredients such as agave are still sugars, and stevia is a better option.

Preparing the cupboards

Now comes the time to bring the cupboards back to life. Sweep them out to remove food particles, then give them a wipe over with an all-purpose natural cleaner such as white vinegar, which will tackle the grease and grime. A solution of half vinegar and half water will remove build-up, but for stubborn dirt you can use the vinegar neat. Bicarbonate of soda (baking soda) and water is a formidable natural non-abrasive scrub for the kitchen.

When your cupboards are clean, replace the food you are keeping, giving it a quick wipe down. Store loose items in airtight containers. Have one shelf for stockpile foods so it's easy to find a quick snack.

Tackling the fridge and freezer

Now make a start on the fridge and freezer using the same process. Don't let frozen products defrost — keep them in an ice bucket while you are classifying and arranging.

When it comes to food in the fridge and freezer, if in doubt, throw it out. If it looks mouldy, mysterious, unrecognisable, spoilt or smells strange, give it the boot, even if it's within its use-by date. Make sure your fridge is set at 40°C (100°F) or less, and your freezer at 0°C (32°F) or less.

Wrap and enclose food tightly before placing it back in the freezer.

Supercharged shopping

Now that the pantry, fridge and freezer are sorted, it's time to hit the shops. When shopping, a good rule of thumb is to check labels and look for foods as unadulterated as possible — and if the budget allows, always opt for organic.

Within the wide range of foods featured on the shopping list on page 26 you'll have many opportunities to try out foods, experiment and pull together a wide variety of delicious and nutritious meals in a pinch.

7-day meal planner

Walk through the sample meal plan opposite using it as a guide when planning your healthy recipes for the week. When customising your own meal plan, aim to balance meals nutritionally so that you have a good ratio of healthy ingredients and foods are being rotated.

Now it's time to go *au naturel* and start creating a whole new world of knock-your-socks-off nosh. Let your imagination run wild and have a great time experimenting in the kitchen.

 Supercharged tip Why not try a different type of vegetable like daikon, or a new kind of breakfast cereal like buckwheat? By tasting new foods you'll be able to add plenty of new favourites to your own supercharged shopping list.

	Breakfast	Lunch	Dinner
Monday	• Warm water with lemon • Spinach Toast with avocado, tomato & basil • Supercharged Shake	• Crispy Baked Herb-Encrusted Salmon with wilted Spinach • Peppermint tea	• Beef steak with green beans, Crunchy Daikon Chips and squash mash • Dairy-free Coconut, Almond & Vanilla Ice Cream • Chamomile tea
Tuesday	• Decaffeinated coffee (Swiss water-processed) • Buckwheat Pancakes with Blueberry Compote • Supercharged Shake	• Fabulous Fishy Burger with three-leaf salad and Mayonnaise • Green Renewal Juice	• Shepherd's Pie with Cauliflower Mash & steamed greens • Vanilla Custard • Lavender Tea with Almond Milk
Wednesday	• Peppermint tea • Spangled Eggs with Lemon, Basil & Tomato • Supercharged Shake	• Zucchini & Celery Nut Loaf • Dandelion tea	• Lamburgers with Rosemary, Antioxidant Salad and Turnip Chips • Banana & Coconut Muffin • Ginger tea
Thursday	• Warm water with lemon • Buckwheat Porridge with Cinnamon-Toasted Almonds • Tropical Blueberry Smoothie	• Caramelised Onion & Rosemary Frittata • Broccoli & Red Onion Salad • Green Renewal Juice	• Autumn Braised Vegetables • Almond & Zucchini Bread with Cashew Nut Cream • Mint & Ginger Tisane
Friday	• Cucumber, Tomato & Basil Detox • Poached Eggs on Super Seeded Bread with Smoked Salmon & Hollandaise • Supercharged Shake	• Stacked Prawn & Avocado Salad with Lee's Jam Jar Dressing • Ginger tea	• Zingy Lemon Pesto with Oomph with Aromatic Herb & Garlic Crackers • Vegetable Soup on a Cold Night • Coconut & Almond Bliss Balls • Lemon balm tea
Saturday	• Warm water with lemon	• **Cafe breakfast:** poached eggs, nitrate-free bacon, spinach and avocado • Herbal tea	• Bollywood Bombay Chicken Curry with brown rice • Gluten-Free Nut Loaf • Hibiscus tea
Sunday	• Dandelion Chai Latte • Toasted Almond & Zucchini Bread with avocado & nut butter	• **Sunday roast:** Organic lamb leg, squash mash, green beans and Crunchy Daikon Chips • Dandelion Chai Latte	• Creamy Cauliflower & Turnip Soup • Butternut Cookies • Peppermint tea

drinks
& milks

Green renewal juice

If supplements make your skin crawl, I recommend investing in a juicer or asking your local juice bar or fruit and vegetable store to make up an invigorating green juice for you. Green juices don't need to be hard-core and unpalatable to do their job. This is one of my favourite enzyme-rich green juices — perfect for eliminating toxins and free radicals. It's quick and easy to make, and you'll probably find all the ingredients in your vegetable crisper.

1 bunch (about 350 g/12 oz)
   English spinach
1 handful mint
1 handful parsley
1 tablespoon lemon juice
1 Lebanese (short) cucumber,
   cut in half lengthways
a few lettuce leaves
4 celery stalks
2–3 cm (³/₄–1¹/₄ inch) knob of
   fresh ginger, peeled
6 ice cubes

With the motor running, feed all the ingredients except the ice cubes into a juicer one at a time. Pour into a drinking glass, add the ice cubes and sip slowly to enjoy its benefits.

Serves 1

 Supercharged tip I occasionally use kale in this juice for added fireworks. It gives extra bite, so it's not for the faint-hearted. Start with one leaf and work your way up. I also like to plonk the whole lemon in, peel and all. Try this once you are familiar with the flavour.

Cucumber, tomato & basil detox

Juicing is a wonderful way to ensure you are consuming your recommended servings of greens. Unless you're Popeye, no one wants to eat three bunches of spinach and four cucumbers at 7 am, but juicing enables us to get a healthy amount of vegetables in one go to power-up the day. Juiced greens are rich in chlorophyll, which helps oxygenate the body, neutralise the pollution that we breathe in and release stored toxins in our bodies.

1 large Lebanese (short) cucumber,
   cut in half lengthways
1 large handful basil leaves
3 tomatoes, halved
1 lime, peeled
6 ice cubes

With the motor running, feed the cucumber, basil, tomatoes and lime into a juicer one at a time. Put the ice cubes in a glass, pour the juice and drink immediately.

Serves 1

 Health benefit: Basil is an excellent source of magnesium, chlorophyll, iron, calcium and vitamins C and A. It's a wonderful detoxer and an anti-inflammatory agent, too.

Supercharged shake

Breakfast is the best time to indulge in this fortifying shake, full of essential nutrients to kick-start the day. Combine it with good fats and the nutrients will absorb faster. Along with the shake I take the following supplements to boost my immune system: a vitamin B multi, 1 tablespoon cod liver oil, 5000 IU vitamin D and 400 IU vitamin E. If you do decide to take supplements, make sure they are non-synthetic and free of additives and sugars. I take the shake from Monday to Friday and give my body a rest on the weekend.

250 ml (9 fl oz/1 cup) filtered water or
  Silky Smooth Almond Milk (see page 38)
1 organic egg (optional)
600 mg calcium citrate powder
600 mg magnesium citrate powder
1 teaspoon dairy-free probiotic powder
1 teaspoon vitamin C powder with
  bioflavonoids

Place all the ingredients in a blender and blend until smooth. Pour into a tall glass and enjoy this perfect pick-me-up. Bottoms up!

Serves 1

Mint & ginger tisane

Soothe your soul with this powerful, calming herbal infusion. If you suffer from ulcerative colitis, ginger will help to reduce inflammation and soothe the intestinal tract; it's also a wonder for alleviating nausea and travel sickness. The addition of mint softens the ginger so it doesn't come off too spicy.

2.5 cm (1 inch) knob of fresh ginger, peeled and sliced
1 handful mint leaves
625 ml (21½ fl oz/2½ cups) boiling filtered water
liquid stevia or stevia powder, to taste

Put the ginger in a freshly warmed teapot and add the mint. Carefully pour the water into the teapot, put the lid on and leave to steep for 5 minutes. Add stevia to taste.

Drink warm, or chilled with ice cubes.

Serves 2

Lemon, garlic & ginger elixir

Mix up this magical concoction to combat winter chills and keep bugs at bay. It is best served hot.

2 tablespoons lemon juice
2 teaspoons crushed garlic
5 cm (2 inch) knob of fresh ginger, peeled and grated
2 tablespoons apple cider vinegar
500 ml (17 fl oz/2 cups) filtered water
liquid stevia or stevia powder, to taste

Place the lemon juice, garlic, ginger and vinegar in a teapot. Bring the water to a rapid boil, then carefully pour it into the teapot, put the lid on and leave to steep for a few minutes. Add stevia to taste.

Strain into mugs and enjoy immediately.

Serves 2

 Health benefit: Brimming with beneficial enzymes, apple cider vinegar is a natural antibacterial, blood oxidiser and purifying agent. It can be used as a dressing to pucker-up salads, it can be sprinkled over steamed vegetables or mixed with water as a wonderful health tonic. The unfiltered version, which appears slightly cloudy, has the most health benefits. The sediment will collect at the bottom, so shake the bottle before use. It is best refrigerated.

Silky smooth almond milk

Reassuringly simple, containing no animal hormones, antibiotics or chemicals found in regular cow's milk, almond milk is a nutritious and fibre-rich non-dairy alternative. Almond milk will stay fresh in the fridge for up to six days. You can use it as a stand-in to create dairy-free dessert recipes, over cereal, in drinks and in baking. If almonds aren't your thing, try substituting them with hazelnuts.

750 ml (26 fl oz/3 cups) filtered water, boiled, then cooled slightly
160 g (5¾ oz/1 cup) blanched or soaked almonds (see tip below)
liquid stevia or stevia powder, to taste

Put the water and almonds in a blender and whirl until smooth. Place a fine sieve over a jug and pour in the almond milk, reserving the almond pulp left in the sieve. Sweeten the almond milk with stevia to taste.

Transfer the liquid to a sterilised milk bottle, then cover and keep refrigerated.

The reserved almond pulp can be used to make ice cream (see Dairy-free Coconut, Almond & Vanilla Ice Cream, page 168), desserts or spreads, or you can make more almond milk by adding the almond pulp to the blender with more water (this can be done up to three times). The almond pulp will keep in a sealed container in the fridge for up to 3 days.

Makes 550 ml (19 fl oz/2½ cups)

 Supercharged tip I like to use blanched almonds because they give a good creamy white colour, but you can also blanch almond kernels at home. Put 160 g (5¾ oz/1 cup) raw almond kernels in a bowl of filtered warm water, add 1 teaspoon sea salt and leave overnight. The next day, drain the almonds and pat them dry with paper towels. Discard the skins.

Lavender tea with almond milk

Something about this tea speaks to me. I have to literally hold myself back from downing it in one go. There's nothing more delectable than a lavender tea after an exhausting day. With its delicate floral scent, this tea creates the perfect moment to unwind and enjoy its fragrant, flowery goodness. An antidote to insomnia, drink it before bed and you'll be guaranteed a relaxing night's sleep. Once you have tried this tea you'll be able to adjust the quantity of lavender to taste.

1 handful dried lavender blossoms
250 ml (9 fl oz/1 cup) boiling filtered water
125 ml (4 fl oz/½ cup) Silky Smooth
    Almond Milk (see page 38), warmed

Place the lavender blossoms in a warmed teapot and pour the water over the top. Cover with the lid and allow to steep for 7 minutes.

Add the almond milk, strain into a mug, then sip and count your blessings.

Serves 1

Homemade coconut milk

You don't have to reside among swaying palm trees and idyllic tropical surrounds
to enjoy the delicious health benefits of luxurious coconut milk. Bringing the taste
of an island paradise to your table is as simple as sauntering around the South Pacific.
Too easy. You can also use this recipe to make a thick coconut cream, by using 220 g
(7¾ oz/4 cups) coconut flakes to 250 ml (9 fl oz/1 cup) filtered water.

**500 ml (17 fl oz/2 cups) filtered water,
boiled, then cooled slightly
110 g (3¾ oz/2 cups) coconut flakes**

Put the water and coconut flakes in a blender and process
until smooth. Place a fine sieve over a jug and pour the
coconut milk in, pressing it through firmly. Reserve the
coconut pulp remaining in the sieve.

Pour the coconut milk from the jug into a sterilised milk
bottle, then cover and keep refrigerated. The coconut milk
will keep for up to a week.

The reserved coconut pulp can be used to make creamy
ice cream, desserts or spreads, and can be added to
smoothies and baked goods. It also adds extra creaminess,
texture and depth to Thai dishes and curries.

Makes about 550 ml (19 fl oz)

Egg milk

**3 organic eggs
1 litre (35 fl oz/4 cups) warm or cold
filtered water
about 4 drops liquid stevia (optional)**

Break the eggs into a blender. With the motor running
on low speed, gradually add the water. If you like a sweet
milk, add stevia to taste.

Pour into a large jar or container, then cover and
refrigerate for up to 5 days. Enjoy cold as a pick-me-up.

Makes about 1 litre (35 fl oz/4 cups)

Dandelion chai latte

If you're detoxing from caffeine but still want to enjoy a latte, why not try a steaming cup of fragrant dandy chai? Ginger and cinnamon make it a healthy digestive, and even though it's dairy and sugar-free you won't be compromising on sweetness and flavour. It's the perfect warm drink for a Sunday afternoon curled up on the couch with a good book.

3 cardamom pods
1 star anise
4 cloves
500 ml (17 fl oz/2 cups) Silky Smooth
   Almond Milk (see page 38)
5 drops liquid stevia
2 dandelion tea bags (lactose free)
5 cm (2 inch) knob of fresh ginger,
   peeled and thinly sliced
1 cinnamon stick
a pinch of grated nutmeg

Crush the cardamom, star anise and cloves lightly with the back of a spoon. Place in a saucepan and add the almond milk and stevia. Bring to the boil, reduce the heat to low and simmer for 5 minutes.

Remove the saucepan from the heat and add the tea bags, ginger and cinnamon. Stir gently. Cover the pan and let the chai steep for 3 minutes. Strain, then allow to cool slightly. If you have a hand-held milk frother, now is the time to get frothing.

Pour the chai into your favourite mug, sprinkle a little nutmeg on top and slowly sip.

Serves 2

 Supercharged tip Dandelion tea is a wonderful liver detoxer.

Tropical blueberry smoothie

On those mornings when you're in a mad rush to get out the door, this smoothie can be slurped down or made to go as a filling, liquid meal replacement or in-between snack. You can adjust the amount of almond and coconut milk you use, depending upon the desired consistency. If you prefer chunky bursts of blueberry goodness on your tongue, shorten your blending time. You'll buzz with vitality until lunchtime.

375 ml (13 fl oz/1½ cups) Silky Smooth
  Almond Milk (see page 38)
125 ml (4 fl oz/½ cup) Homemade
  Coconut Milk (see page 44)
80 g (2¾ oz/½ cup) fresh or frozen
  blueberries
1 teaspoon finely grated lemon zest
1 tablespoon lemon juice
¼ teaspoon liquid stevia or stevia powder
5 ice cubes
coconut flakes, to serve

Place all the ingredients in a blender and blend until smooth. Pour into two tall glasses and serve with a sprinkling of coconut flakes.

Serves 2

breakfast

Buckwheat pancakes with blueberry compote

I'm wild about blueberries. Packed with antioxidants, which fight free radicals in the body, they build up your immunity and have unique healing properties. Blueberries are high in fibre, enriched with Vitamin C and can be enjoyed solo or added to smoothies. Pair them with buckwheat pancakes and you'll have double the punch.

65 g (2¼ oz/½ cup) buckwheat flour
1 teaspoon gluten-free baking powder
1 organic egg
5 drops liquid stevia
250 ml (9 fl oz/1 cup) rice milk or Silky
   Smooth Almond Milk (see page 38)
coconut oil, for pan-frying
Cashew Nut Cream (see page 185),
   to serve (optional)

Blueberry compote
150 g (5½ oz) fresh blueberries (or frozen
   blueberries with no added sugar)
2 tablespoons filtered water
5 drops liquid stevia
½ teaspoon natural vanilla extract
a pinch of sea salt

In a large jug, mix the flour and baking powder well. Add the egg, stevia and milk and whisk to remove any lumps. Leave for 10 minutes to settle.

Meanwhile, put all the blueberry compote ingredients in a small saucepan and bring to the boil over medium–high heat. Reduce the heat to low and simmer gently for about 10 minutes, stirring often. Keep warm while making the pancakes.

Pour a light coating of coconut oil into a frying pan and place over high heat. Carefully pour in one-eighth of the batter, swirling it in the pan to make a thin layer. Reduce the heat slightly and when the underside of the pancake is browned, flip it over to brown the other side. Remove from the pan and keep warm while making seven more pancakes from the remaining batter, oiling the pan with more coconut oil as needed.

Serve the pancakes with warm blueberry compote and topped with a dollop of Cashew Nut Cream, if desired.

Makes 8 pancakes

 Health benefits Popular in China, buckwheat helps lower blood pressure and cholesterol due to its rich supply of rutin, an antioxidant phytonutrient.

Poached eggs on super seeded bread with smoked salmon & hollandaise

1 teaspoon apple cider vinegar

4 organic eggs

2 slices Super Seeded Bread (see page 175)

4 slices smoked salmon

2 dollops Hollandaise (see page 178)

2 teaspoons nutritional yeast flakes

dill sprigs, to garnish

Bring a shallow saucepan of water to the boil and add the vinegar (to help stop the eggs separating during poaching). Break the eggs one at a time onto a saucer, then slide them carefully into the water. Poach the eggs for several minutes, or until cooked to your liking.

Meanwhile, toast the bread and divide among two plates.

Top each slice of toast with two smoked salmon slices and a dollop of hollandaise. Gently remove the poached eggs from the simmering water with a slotted spoon and place two on each slice of toast.

Serve at once, sprinkled with the yeast flakes and garnished with dill.

Serves 2

 Health tip A fantastic natural flavour enhancer, nutritional yeast flakes are a bright mustard-yellow and loaded with B vitamins, amino acids and minerals. They can be used in cooking, as a condiment, or to make a warm beverage. Unlike traditional yeast, nutritional yeast flakes contain Saccharomyces cerevisiae, so they do not feed candida. You can buy them from health food stores or online.

Almond hotcakes with lemon

3 organic eggs
200 g (7 oz/2 cups) almond meal
2 drops liquid stevia
250 ml (9 fl oz/1 cup) rice milk or Silky
    Smooth Almond Milk (see page 38)
a pinch of sea salt
2 tablespoons extra virgin olive oil
    (or organic butter if tolerated)
stevia powder, to serve
lemon wedges, to serve

Beat the eggs in a bowl, then whisk in the almond meal, stevia, milk and sea salt. Leave for 10 minutes to settle.

Pour a little of the olive oil into a frying pan and place over medium–high heat. Making several hotcakes at a time, spoon in 60 ml (2 fl oz/1/4 cup) of the batter into the pan for each hotcake — you can pour the batter into lightly oiled egg rings for a neater shape, if desired. When the batter has set and is bubbling, about 2–3 minutes, carefully flip the hotcakes over and cook them on the other side. Remove from the pan and keep warm.

Heat a little more olive oil in the pan and cook the remaining batter in the same way.

Serve the hotcakes warm, sprinkled with stevia powder and accompanied by lemon wedges.

Makes 8

Supercharged muesli

75 g (2½ oz/½ cup) pepitas
    (pumpkin seeds)
75 g (2½ oz/½ cup) sunflower seeds
90 g (3¼ oz/½ cup) Activated Sea Salt
    and Vinegar Almonds (see page 70)
50 g (1¾ oz/½ cup) LSA mix (mixed
    crushed linseeds, sunflower seeds
    and almonds)
30 g (1 oz/½ cup) buckwheat, brown rice
    or quinoa puffs
1 apple, grated
2–3 tablespoons lemon juice
Silky Smooth Almond Milk (see page 38),
    to serve
coconut flakes, to serve
goji berries, to serve (optional)

Mix the pepitas, sunflower seeds, almonds, LSA and puffs together and divide among two bowls. Mix the apple through each bowl and add lemon juice to taste.

Add the desired amount of almond milk, then sprinkle with coconut flakes, and goji berries if using. Enjoy.

Serves 2

Buckwheat porridge with cinnamon toasted almonds

My first encounter with buckwheat was a strange one. I couldn't get my head around the fact that it is called buckwheat, but it isn't actually wheat at all — it is in fact a member of the rhubarb family. Characterised by its triangular shape, the outer hull is removed to make it edible. You can buy it unroasted or roasted (under the name 'kasha') and the tastes do vary. Ground into flour, it can be used in baking, bread making, decadent muffins and pancakes. Adding brown rice flour or almond meal when baking enhances buckwheat's ability to produce gorgeously smooth baked goods.

225 g (8 oz/1 cup) roasted buckwheat
   groats
50 g (1³/4 oz/¹/2 cup) flaked almonds
¹/3 teaspoon ground cinnamon
1 organic egg, beaten
2 tablespoons coconut oil (or butter
   if tolerated)
500 ml (17 fl oz/2 cups) Silky Smooth
   Almond Milk (see page 38)
¹/2 teaspoon sea salt
6 drops liquid stevia

Rinse the buckwheat groats under cold water and set aside in a bowl.

In a dry frying pan over medium heat, lightly toast the almonds with a sprinkling of the cinnamon, stirring often and keeping a close watch to ensure they don't burn. Transfer to a small bowl to cool. Add the egg and remaining cinnamon to the buckwheat and mix well.

Heat the coconut oil in a saucepan over medium heat and add the buckwheat mixture. Stir for several minutes, or until the buckwheat has dried out and separated.

In another saucepan, bring the almond milk to the boil. Stir 375 ml (13 fl oz/1¹/2 cups) of the almond milk into the buckwheat mixture and keep the remaining almond milk warm.

When the buckwheat mixture has returned to the boil, add the sea salt and stevia. Reduce the heat to low and simmer, covered, for 10–15 minutes, or until the buckwheat is soft but not mushy.

Spoon the buckwheat into two bowls, then stir the cinnamon almonds and remaining almond milk through. Serve hot.

Serves 2

Quinoa with almond milk

Who needs styrofoam-tasting packet cereals when you are good to go with a wonderfully hearty breakfast in around 12 minutes? Quinoa for breakfast is tasty and delicious — fluffy, nutty and delicate in flavour. Add almond milk to the proceedings and you'll be fuelling your body with essential protein, giving you energy to spare to sail through the day with no grumbly hunger pangs.

200 g (7 oz/1 cup) quinoa
¼ teaspoon sea salt
½ teaspoon ground cinnamon
6 drops liquid stevia
1 tablespoon coconut oil (or melted
  organic butter, if tolerated)
Silky Smooth Almond Milk (see page 38),
  to serve

Bring 500 ml (17 fl oz/2 cups) filtered water to the boil in a wide saucepan. Stir in the quinoa, salt, cinnamon, stevia and coconut oil. Cover, reduce the heat and simmer gently for 12 minutes.

Scoop the mixture into a bowl and add almond milk to taste. Enjoy hot or at room temperature.

Serves 2

 Supercharged tip Quinoa comes in different colours and varieties, from ivory to pink, brown to red and jet black. When cooking quinoa you'll notice that the outer casing will twist around and form a tiny ivory spirally tail — this is what gives it a distinct crunch.

Spangled eggs with lemon, basil & tomato

When my daughter Tamsin (who's nearly 16) was younger, she got into the habit of calling these scrambled eggs 'spangled eggs', and we've called them this ever since. The secret to making great spangled eggs is to add lemon zest to the mix. It gives a tremendous citrus burst in the mouth and adds a richer flavour. Pile the clouds of egg high and garnish with fresh basil leaves and juicy cherry tomatoes.

3 organic eggs
1 tablespoon filtered water
sea salt, to taste
1 tablespoon extra virgin olive oil
1 teaspoon finely grated lemon zest
10 basil leaves
6 cherry tomatoes, halved
extra virgin olive oil, for drizzling

In a bowl, whisk the eggs and water together until light and fluffy, then add sea salt to taste.

Heat the olive oil in a non-stick frying pan over low to medium–low heat. Add the eggs and flick them around the pan with a spatula so they don't stick to the bottom. Now it's time to sprinkle in the lemon zest and extra sea salt if, desired.

Garnish two breakfast plates with basil leaves and tomato halves, and dress with a drop or two of olive oil. Tumble the eggs out onto one side of each plate and serve at once.

Serves 2

Mini frittatas with tomato & rocket

Deliciously simple, mini frittatas are protein-packed and nutrient-rich — after just a few bites you'll feel ready to take on the world. Protein can help you get to that couldn't-eat-another-bite feeling, giving you a no-gorge guarantee for breakfast and morning tea. These versatile breakfast bites are also a great lunchbox idea for kids, work a treat served cold for a light afternoon tea, and make fabulous finger food.

1 tablespoon extra virgin olive oil

1 onion, chopped

6 organic eggs

3 tablespoons Silky Smooth
  Almond Milk (see page 38)

6 vine-ripened cherry tomatoes,
  quartered

1 handful rocket (arugula) or English
  spinach leaves, chopped

Preheat the oven to 175°C (345°F/Gas 4). Grease a 6-hole giant muffin tin (each hole 250 ml/9 fl oz/1 cup capacity).

Heat the olive oil in a frying pan and fry the onion over low heat until caramelised, about 8–10 minutes.

In a bowl, whisk the eggs and almond milk together, then stir in the tomatoes, rocket and caramelised onion. Season with sea salt and freshly ground black pepper.

Divide the mixture among the muffin holes and bake for 20 minutes, or until the frittatas are set. Allow to cool a little before removing from the tray and cooling on a wire rack.

Makes 6

dips & snacks

Roasted eggplant relish

If you love entertaining or you're a born grazer, dips such as this one will become a permanent fixture on your menu. A homemade dip adds the perfect touch to a celebration or gathering and makes a fabulous conversation starter. All of the dips in this book can be prepared well in advance and are so simple to make you won't feel like you're a slave to the kitchen, leaving you free to enjoy the party. This all-round favourite can be served as a dip, side dish or starter and is also delicious tossed through pasta.

1 large eggplant (aubergine)
1 red capsicum (pepper), quartered
200 g (7 oz) grape (baby roma) tomatoes
4 tablespoons extra virgin olive oil
1/2 small onion, diced
1/2 teaspoon ground cumin
1 tablespoon chopped mint
2 teaspoons lemon juice
1/2 tablespoon apple cider vinegar

Preheat the oven to 200°C (400°F/Gas 6). Cut the eggplant into 2–3 cm (3/4–1 1/4 inch) dice. Place on a baking tray with the capsicum and tomatoes, drizzle with half the olive oil and season with sea salt and freshly ground black pepper. Bake for 25 minutes, or until the eggplant is tender and cooked through.

Remove the vegetables from the oven and set aside until cool enough to handle. Remove the skin from the capsicum strips, then chop each strip into 4–6 smaller pieces. Place in a bowl with the eggplant and tomatoes, onion, cumin and mint. Drizzle in the remaining olive oil, the lemon juice and vinegar. Season to taste with sea salt and freshly ground black pepper, then toss to combine.

Using a fork, mix the ingredients together to give a roughly cut, chunky texture. Alternatively, for a smoother relish, blend the mixture in a food processor or blender.

Cover and refrigerate until ready to serve. The relish will keep in a sealed container in the fridge for up to 3 days.

Makes about 500 g (1 lb 2 oz/2 cups)

Oven-roasted pumpkin crisps

The best way to achieve evenly thin pumpkin slices is by using a mandoline, or the slicing blade on your food processor.

½ small pumpkin (winter squash)
extra virgin olive oil, for brushing

Preheat the oven to 150°C (300°F/Gas 2). Cut the pumpkin into two or three chunks, then peel, if desired, and seed each chunk. Using a mandoline or the slicing blade on your food processor, cut the chunks into very thin slices, about 2 mm (1/16 inch) thick. Dry the slices on paper towels. The tail ends and odd sizes can be used for other recipes, such as mashed pumpkin.

Place the pumpkin slices in a single layer on two lined baking trays. Brush with olive oil and sprinkle with a good pinch of sea salt. The salt helps draw moisture from the vegetables, so let them sit for 5 minutes before placing in the oven.

Bake the pumpkin slices for 25 minutes, or until crisp and golden.

Remove from the oven to cool completely — the slices will crisp up as they cool. The crisps will stay fresh in an airtight container for up to 2 weeks.

Makes lots!

Supercharged tip If you're ever buying commercially prepared vegie crisps, check the packet for added flours such as corn and potato, along with artificial colourings and flavourings.

Activated sea salt & vinegar almonds

Everyone who tries these almonds tells me they taste exactly like salt and vinegar chips, an old favourite of mine. They'll kick your tastebuds in an intoxicating way, and I can't recommend them highly enough as a delicious and healthy in-between snack. Sprinkling them with a good splosh of apple cider vinegar before baking makes them a natural metabolism and immune-system booster. Trick or treat? Definitely treat!

320 g (11¼ oz/2 cups) raw almond kernels
3 tablespoons apple cider vinegar
2 teaspoons sea salt

Soak the almonds overnight in a bowl of filtered water with ½ teaspoon sea salt. This makes them super-easy to digest.

The next day, preheat the oven to 50°C (120°F/Gas ¼), or as low as your oven will go. Drain and rinse the almonds, then dry them off well with paper towels.

Spread the almonds on a baking tray, then sprinkle with the vinegar and sea salt. Bake for 5½–6 hours, or until golden brown, moving them around the tray every now and then with long-handled tongs so they toast evenly.

Remove from the oven and allow to cool. The almonds will keep in an airtight container for up to 6 months, or even a year.

Makes 350 g (12 oz/2 cups)

Zingy lemon pesto with oomph

Guests will quiver with excitement when they find out the good news: a wheat, gluten, dairy, yeast, sugar and additive-free starter that tastes superb! The sweetness and pungency of the basil combined with the tart zing of sparkly lemon zest makes this dip worth taking the plunge. Get on it.

3 cups basil leaves
2 small garlic cloves, crushed
1 tablespoon lemon juice
4 tablespoons pine nuts
1 tablespoon nutritional yeast flakes
3–4 tablespoons extra virgin olive oil

Put the basil, garlic, lemon juice, pine nuts and yeast flakes in a blender or food processor and whiz until puréed. With the motor running, gradually add as much olive oil as needed to give a silky but spoonable texture. Season with sea salt and freshly ground black pepper.

If you're not using the pesto straightaway, spoon it into an airtight container, pour a thin layer of olive oil over the pesto to cover it, then seal the lid on tightly. The pesto will then keep well in the fridge for up to 4 days.

Makes about 125 g (4¹/2 oz/¹/2 cup)

 Supercharged tip Smart snacking works. Eating small, nutritious meals throughout the day can help keep energy levels up so you won't be tempted to haphazardly scoff down a ghoulish amount of ho-hum potato chips or pretzels, washed down with a sugary drink. Having a few bites mid-morning or mid-afternoon is a sound way to stabilise blood sugar levels, so you won't be caught on the blood sugar rollercoaster that can leave you trembling, anxious, weak and irritable.

Olive tapenade

150 g (5½ oz) pitted black olives
6 basil leaves
2 garlic cloves, coarsely chopped
3 anchovy fillets
1 teaspoon capers, rinsed
1 tablespoon chopped parsley
1 teaspoon lemon juice
3 tablespoons extra virgin olive oil

Place the olives, basil, garlic, anchovies, capers, parsley and lemon juice in a food processor and whiz to a paste. With the motor running, slowly add the olive oil until the desired consistency is reached. Add freshly ground black pepper to taste.

Cover and refrigerate until ready to serve. The tapenade will keep in an airtight container in the fridge for a week.

Makes 250 g (9 oz/1 cup)

Chicken liver pâté

3 tablespoons extra virgin olive oil
500 g (1 lb 2 oz) organic chicken livers
1 onion, finely chopped
2 teaspoons finely grated lemon zest
½ teaspoon sea salt
1 teaspoon finely chopped rosemary
1 teaspoon finely chopped thyme
2 garlic cloves, crushed
a generous pinch of grated nutmeg

Heat the olive oil in a frying pan over medium heat. Add the chicken livers and onion and sauté for about 10 minutes, or until the livers are lightly browned, with no pink remaining.

Transfer the mixture to a food processor, add the remaining ingredients and season well with freshly ground black pepper. Process until light and smooth.

Transfer to a small pot, cover with a lid and place in the fridge to chill before using, to allow the flavours to blend. The pâté will keep for several days.

Serves 4–6

Aromatic herb & garlic crackers

Made from just a handful of ingredients yet still positively gourmet, these totally gluten and sugar-free snacks are a perfect stand-in for traditional crackers. Top them with avocado and tomato or a dip from this book and you're good to go.

125 g (4½ oz/1¼ cups) almond meal
½ teaspoon sea salt
80 g (2¾ oz/½ cup) sesame seeds
1½ teaspoons finely chopped mixed herbs
2 garlic cloves, crushed
1 organic egg
1½ tablespoons extra virgin olive oil

Preheat the oven to 175ºC (345ºF/Gas 4) and grease a baking tray.

Combine the almond meal, salt, sesame seeds, herbs and garlic in a bowl. Whisk the egg in a small jug, then slowly whisk in the olive oil. Pour the egg mixture into the dry ingredients and mix to combine, then knead the mixture with your hands to form a smooth dough. If necessary, mix in a little water to bring it together.

Roll the dough out on a sheet of baking paper to a thin rectangle measuring about 35 x 25 cm (14 x 10 inches). Trim the edges.

Place the prepared baking tray face-down over the dough, then invert the two together so the dough is now on the top. Peel off the baking paper.

Using a sharp knife, cut the dough into 5 cm (2 inch) squares. Bake for 12–15 minutes, or until golden, turning the crackers over halfway through. Remove from the oven and allow to cool completely before serving.

The crackers will stay fresh in an airtight container at room temperature for up to 2 days.

Makes about 35 crackers

Pesto-filled zucchini flowers

A *wonderful* starter, these captivating, eye-catching flowers will have your guests smitten. Zucchini flowers are surprisingly versatile: they can be sautéed, roasted or steamed, or chopped and added to frittatas and stir-fries. I love to stuff them with dairy-free pesto for a mouth-watering bliss bomb. You can prepare them earlier in the day, then sauté them at the last minute when guests arrive, or snack pangs strike.

Dairy-free pesto

3 cups basil leaves

2 small garlic cloves, crushed

1 tablespoon lemon juice

2 tablespoons extra virgin olive oil

4 tablespoons pine nuts

1 tablespoon nutritional yeast flakes

Batter

120 g (4¼ oz/¾ cup) brown rice flour

250 ml (9 fl oz/1 cup) chilled soda water (club soda)

16 zucchini (courgette) flowers

grape seed oil, for pan-frying

lemon wedges, to serve (optional)

Put all the pesto ingredients in a blender or food processor and whiz until puréed. Add sea salt and freshly ground black pepper to taste.

To make the batter, put the flour in a bowl and gradually mix in the soda water until the batter resembles a pancake mix — not too thick and not too runny. Set aside.

Gently open the petals of a zucchini flower and remove the stamen from the centre. Repeat with the remaining flowers, then chop 2–3 cm (¾–1¼ inches) from the end of each stem. Spoon 1 teaspoon of the pesto inside each flower, then gently twist the petals closed.

Pour grape seed oil into a frying pan to a depth of 3 cm (1¼ inches) and place over medium heat. Working two or three at a time, dip the zucchini flowers in the batter, shake off the excess, then carefully drop into the hot oil. Fry briefly until golden on all sides.

Remove the zucchini flowers with a slotted spoon and place on paper towels to drain. Serve at once with lemon wedges.

Makes 16

Crunchy daikon rolls

I love these rolls. They are a wonderfully healthy, fresh-tasting alternative to those traditional deep-fried spring roll temptations that endlessly follow you around at social gatherings or events. You'll love the combination of flavours in these healthy show-stoppers — from the sharpness of the apple cider vinegar to the zestiness of lime, compounded with sweet capsicum and minty leaves.

1 large daikon, peeled
2 tablespoons lemon juice
2 spring onions (scallions), sliced
   lengthways
1 Lebanese (short) cucumber,
   peeled and julienned
2–3 cm (³/₄–1¹/₄ inch) knob of fresh
   ginger, peeled and julienned
1 long yellow capsicum (pepper),
   julienned
1 long red capsicum (pepper),
   julienned
60 g (2¹/₄ oz/¹/₂ cup) snow pea
   (mangetout) sprouts
115 g (4 oz/1 cup) bean sprouts
1 large handful coriander
   (cilantro) leaves
1 handful mint leaves
1 tablespoon wheat-free tamari
3 tablespoons apple cider vinegar
¹/₂ teaspoon sesame oil
1 tablespoon lime juice
1 red chilli, thinly sliced (optional)

Using a vegetable peeler, slice the daikon lengthways into very thin slices, measuring about 5 x 10 cm (2 x 4 inches) — if you have one, a mandoline is great for this. Add the lemon juice to a bowl of warm water and soak the daikon strips in the water for 20 minutes to soften them enough for rolling.

Meanwhile, put the remaining ingredients in a bowl and gently toss together. Leave to marinate for 10 minutes.

Drain the water from the daikon and pat the strips dry with paper towels. Drain the vegetables, reserving the marinade.

Take one daikon strip and place a small amount of the vegetable mixture at the bottom. Roll the daikon strip up with your hands to firmly enclose the filling.

Make more rolls using the remaining daikon and filling, arranging them on an elegant platter as you go.

Pour the marinade into a small bowl and serve as a dipping sauce alongside the rolls. Wait for the ooohs and aaahs!

Makes 20 or more

Health benefits Daikon is a large, mild-flavoured radish that looks like a long, fat white carrot. A mainstay of traditional Japanese cuisine, it is a sweet and pungent tonic for the lungs and liver. Daikon can be boiled or mashed, or used raw in salads. Fresh daikon contains diuretics, decongestants and the digestive enzymes diastase, amylase and esterase, making it beneficial for digestion. It has also proven to be an effective aid against bacterial and fungal infections.

Holy guacamole

As easy as pie to rustle up, guacamole is a wise dip option. Avocado contains significant amounts of heart-healthy essential fatty acids and monounsaturated fats, which help control cholesterol levels and also promote mental acuity — perfect if you want to stay on the ball.

2 avocados, mashed

4 spring onions (scallions), thinly sliced

1 large tomato, finely diced

2 garlic cloves, crushed

3 tablespoons lemon juice

1 small handful coriander (cilantro) leaves, finely chopped

1 tablespoon lime juice

Place all the ingredients in a bowl and season with sea salt and freshly ground black pepper. Mix together thoroughly, then cover and refrigerate until ready to serve.

The guacamole will keep for up to 2 days in the fridge.

Serves 3–4

soups & salads

Vegetable soup on a cold night

2 tablespoons coconut oil

1 onion, diced

2 garlic cloves, crushed

3 celery stalks, diced

140 g (5 oz) sugar-free tomato paste (concentrated purée)

400 g (14 oz) tin chopped tomatoes (sugar and additive free)

150 g (5½ oz) green beans, topped, tailed and cut into 3–4 cm (1¼–1½ inch) lengths

¼ cabbage, coarsely shredded

½ cauliflower, roughly chopped

2 zucchini (courgettes), diced

1 red capsicum (pepper), diced

1 green capsicum (pepper), diced

1 bunch kale or ½ bunch silverbeet (Swiss chard), stalks trimmed and leaves coarsely shredded

1 litre (35 fl oz/4 cups) additive-free vegetable stock or filtered water

1 handful herbs, such as parsley, thyme, rosemary and basil, chopped

Heat the coconut oil in a large heavy-based saucepan and lightly brown the onion, garlic and celery over medium heat for about 5 minutes. Stir in the tomato paste and chopped tomatoes and cook for a minute or two.

Add the beans, cabbage, cauliflower, zucchini, capsicums and kale, and cook for 1–2 minutes more. Add the stock or water and, if necessary pour, in enough extra filtered water to cover the vegetables.

Bring to the boil, reduce the heat and simmer for 1 hour. If you prefer a smoother soup, transfer to a blender or use a hand-held blender and whiz until the desired texture is reached.

Serve hot, sprinkled with the herbs.

Serves 6–8

Thai sweet & sour fish soup

1 litre (35 fl oz/4 cups) Homemade
  Chicken Stock (see page 183) or
  additive-free vegetable stock
2 tablespoons fish sauce
5 cm (2 inch) knob of fresh ginger,
  peeled and sliced
2 garlic cloves, thinly sliced
2 lemongrass stems, white part only,
  cut into 5 cm (2 inch) lengths
5 kaffir lime leaves
liquid stevia, to taste
200 g (7 oz) white fish fillets,
  cut into bite-sized pieces
1 tablespoon lime juice
1 teaspoon grated lime zest
1 small handful mint leaves
2 green chillies, thinly sliced
2 red chillies, thinly sliced

Place the stock, fish sauce, ginger, garlic, lemongrass and four of the kaffir lime leaves in a large saucepan and bring to the boil. Reduce the heat and simmer for 10 minutes. Add a few drops of stevia to taste.

Strain the soup into a large bowl so the soup is now clear. Wipe out the saucepan with a paper towel and return the soup to the pan.

Add the fish, lime juice and lime zest and bring back to the boil. Reduce the heat and simmer for 5 minutes, or until the fish is just cooked. Meanwhile, shred the remaining lime leaf.

Ladle the soup into two serving bowls. Serve hot, garnished with the mint, sliced chillies and shredded kaffir lime leaf.

Serves 2

 Supercharged tip I make my own fish sauce by blitzing 6 anchovies, 3 tablespoons filtered water and 4 drops of liquid stevia in a blender.

Going-green broccoli soup

This grounding green soup is one of my go-to dishes when I feel like I'm flagging and in need of a broccoli boost. You can include the broccoli stems for added nutrients, antioxidants and punch power. I love to make a big batch of this soup and pop it in the freezer to have on nights when I'm looking for instant, nutritious comfort food.

2 tablespoons coconut oil
1 onion, chopped
2 garlic cloves, coarsely chopped
2 celery stalks, chopped
2 heads of broccoli (stems included),
   roughly chopped
500 ml (17 fl oz/2 cups) additive-free
   vegetable stock
1 handful mint leaves, coarsely chopped
1 handful parsley, coarsely chopped
3 tablespoons Homemade Coconut Milk
   (see page 44), optional
slivered almonds, to serve

Heat the coconut oil in a large heavy-based saucepan and sauté the onion and garlic over medium–low heat until the onion becomes translucent, about 5–6 minutes.

Throw in the celery and cook for a minute or two, then add the broccoli and pour the stock in. Bring to the boil, then reduce the heat to a simmer. Add the mint and parsley, season with sea salt and simmer for 15 minutes.

Transfer the soup to a blender. Add the coconut milk, if using, then blend until smooth. If necessary, pour the soup back into the pan and gently reheat it.

Ladle into bowls, scatter each with a few slivered almonds and serve hot.

Serves 4

Creamy cauliflower & turnip soup

I love experimenting with vegetables, and cauliflower is one of my favourites due to its anti-inflammatory properties. It has a mellow flavour, but the trick is to spice it up when the time is right and get those florets tap-dancing in your mouth. Cumin, cinnamon and coriander go well with cauliflower, and it's fabulous in Indian cuisine. This cream-less soup hits the spot for a chilled-out night in. Although earthy and mild in flavour, it still manages to be melt-in-the-mouth sweet and creamy. This healthy soup is rich and satisfying and beats commercially made soup any day. It is best served hot, but also good chilled.

2 tablespoons extra virgin olive oil

1 large onion, chopped

2 garlic cloves, crushed

3 celery stalks, chopped

1 cauliflower, roughly chopped

2 small turnips, peeled and chopped

1 teaspoon grated fresh ginger

2 tablespoons nutritional yeast flakes

1 handful parsley

1 teaspoon sea salt

1/4 teaspoon freshly ground black pepper

750 ml (26 fl oz/3 cups) Homemade Chicken Stock (see page 183) or filtered water

Heat the olive oil in a large heavy-based saucepan and sauté the onion, garlic and celery over medium heat until well coated with the oil, about 1 minute. Add the cauliflower and turnips, reduce the heat to low and cook, stirring often, for 10 minutes.

Stir in the ginger, yeast flakes, parsley, salt and pepper. Pour in the stock and bring to the boil, stirring a couple of times. Reduce the heat, cover and simmer for 20 minutes, or until the vegetables are tender.

Transfer the soup to a blender or use a hand-held blender to whiz the soup to a purée. If necessary, return the soup to the pan to gently reheat before serving.

Serves 2

Chilled-out cucumber & avocado soup

Cucumbers are the perfect summer food, refreshing and mellow, sweet and perfectly light. Even nibbling on them as a snack is a powerful thirst-quencher. Combined with cholesterol-lowering avocado, this soup is a green-goddess, nutrient-rich powerhouse and pairs perfectly with summer fare. It's so simple as there is no cooking involved, and the best way to enjoy it is super-chilled. Leave it for as long as possible in the fridge to encourage the flavours to meld. From the very first spoonful, this soup will make your entire body say aaahhhh.

1 small Lebanese (short) cucumber
3 small avocados
1 handful coriander (cilantro)
1/4 teaspoon ground cumin
1 tablespoon lime juice
1 teaspoon sea salt
500 ml (17 fl oz/2 cups) Homemade
   Chicken Stock (see page 183)
2 spring onions (scallions), thinly sliced,
   to garnish
mint leaves, to serve

Peel the cucumber, cut it in half lengthways and scrape out the seeds. Roughly chop the flesh and place in a blender.

Peel and dice the avocados and add to the blender. Add the coriander, cumin, lime juice, salt and a tablespoon or two of the stock.

Blend the mixture on high speed until puréed. Pour in the remaining stock and blend again until smooth. If necessary, add more stock or some filtered water to thin the soup.

Pour the soup into a bowl, cover with plastic wrap and refrigerate until well chilled.

When you're ready to serve the soup, add sea salt and freshly ground black pepper to taste. Ladle into chilled soup bowls and serve garnished with the spring onion and some mint.

Serves 4

 Health benefits Avocados are a super fruit, loaded with vital nutrients such as vitamins B6, C, E and K, potassium, magnesium and folate, all in a very small package. They're a great source of fibre, and are cholesterol and sodium free. Oleic acid in avocado helps lower blood cholesterol.

Chic French Onion Soup

French onion soup is another really good year-rounder. It's an easy, tasty and wonderfully earthy dish to make. Composed of simple ingredients, the combination of sweet brown onions and hearty beef stock really make this dish soothing and uplifting at the same time.

2 tablespoons olive oil
8 brown onions, thinly sliced
3 garlic cloves, finely chopped
2 litres (70 fl oz/8 cups) Homemade
   Chicken Stock (see page 183), or beef
   stock, or filtered water
1 handful fresh chives, chopped, to serve

Heat the olive oil in a large heavy-based saucepan over medium heat and brown the onions and garlic for about 8–10 minutes. Add the stock or water, cover and bring to the boil. Simmer for about 30 minutes. Add sea salt and freshly ground black pepper to taste. Ladle into wide bowls and serve topped with chopped chives.

Serves 4

Health benefits Onions have significant health benefits, reducing cholesterol and attacking bacteria that cause infection.

Creamy Tomato & Fennel Winter Soup

I grew up on canned tomato soup. In fact, I used to slurp it right out of the can.
But this creamy variation is an entirely different, more sophisticated experience.
After test-driving fennel and adding it with magical results, I have found that it gives
the tomato a helping hand to meld the sweet flavours of the tomatoes and garlic.

2 tablespoons extra virgin olive oil

1 large leek, white part only, sliced

3 garlic cloves, finely chopped

1 red capsicum (pepper), finely chopped

3 celery stalks, thinly sliced

2 small fennel bulbs, finely chopped

1 cup fresh basil leaves

2 x 400 g (14 oz) tins chopped tomatoes
(sugar and additive free)

250 ml (9 fl oz/1 cup) Homemade Tomato
Sauce (see page 181) or tomato passata
(puréed tomatoes)

140 ml (4³/4 fl oz) sugar-free tomato paste
(concentrated purée)

500 ml (17 fl oz/2 cups filtered water
or stock

125 ml (4 fl oz/¹/2 cup) Homemade
Coconut Milk (see page 44)

liquid stevia, to taste

lemon wedges, to serve

Heat the olive oil in a large heavy-based saucepan and
sauté the leek, garlic, capsicum, celery and fennel over
medium heat until softened, about 5 minutes. Add most
of the basil, keeping a few leaves aside for the garnish.
Add the chopped tomatoes, tomato sauce, tomato paste,
water and coconut milk. If necessary, add more filtered
water so that the vegetables are covered. Bring to the
boil, cover and simmer for 45 minutes. Add stevia to
taste. Garnish with reserved basil leaves and serve with
lemon wedges.

Serves 4

Tangy chicken salad with lime dressing

2 handfuls baby English spinach leaves

1/2 yellow capsicum (pepper), diced

50 g (1³/4 oz/1/4 cup) Activated Sea Salt
& Vinegar Almonds (page see 70)

2 celery stalks, thinly sliced

40 g (1¹/2 oz/1/4 cup) sun-dried tomatoes,
sliced

1 Lebanese (short) cucumber, diced

1 avocado, diced

200 g (7 oz) diced oven-roasted chicken

Lime dressing

1 tablespoon apple cider vinegar

1 tablespoon lime juice

1 teaspoon finely grated lime zest

1 garlic clove, crushed

2 tablespoons extra virgin olive oil

Put the spinach, capsicum, almonds, celery, sun-dried tomatoes, cucumber and avocado in a bowl. Toss together gently.

To make the dressing, put the vinegar, lime juice, lime zest and garlic in a small bowl and whisk to combine. Still whisking, drizzle in the olive oil, then add sea salt and freshly ground black pepper to taste.

Spoon the salad onto serving plates and arrange the chicken over the top. Drizzle with the dressing and serve.

Serves 2

Salad niçoise

Salad niçoise is named after Nice, the city in the French Riviera in which it originated. Black olives and anchovies are hallmarks of the region's cuisine, but you can mix and match ingredients depending on your tastes. Full of contrasting flavours, this is an extremely simple recipe, although it's a good idea to prepare the various ingredients before assembling the salad. From the nutritious iron-rich spinach leaves to the vitamin-filled eggs, still soft and jiggly, this salad is a light, yet satisfying, meal — one that could change your life! Bon appétit.

200 g (7 oz) green beans, topped and tailed
2 organic eggs, soft-boiled
2 tablespoons extra virgin olive oil
2 tablespoons lemon juice
100 g (3½ oz/2 cups) baby English
    spinach leaves
2 vine-ripened tomatoes, cut into wedges
8 anchovy fillets, sliced lengthways
175 g (6 oz/1 cup) small black olives
425 g (15 oz) tin tuna in spring water,
    drained and flaked into bite-sized pieces

Cut the beans into 4–5 cm (1½–2 inch) lengths and either steam or blanch them until crispy-tender. Rinse under cold running water to arrest the cooking process and put aside to cool. Peel the eggs and cut them into quarters.

Put the olive oil and lemon juice in a small jar and season lightly with sea salt. Screw the lid on tightly and shake well.

Arrange the spinach leaves on a serving platter and scatter the beans, tomatoes, anchovies and olives around. Tuck the tuna and eggs in and around the salad. Drizzle the dressing over and serve immediately.

Serves 4

Broccoli & red onion salad

This salad is a favourite with everyone who has tried it. Lightly steaming the broccoli makes it more palatable, and the addition of bacon and almonds gives a big hit of flavour. Rich in magnesium, broccoli can be mixed with scrambled eggs or added to salads, soups, sauces and stir-fries. Make this salad at night and take the rest to work for lunch the next day. A force to be reckoned with, it will pep you up and help avoid the mid-afternoon slump.

2 heads of broccoli
4 bacon slices (nitrate and sugar free)
10 spring onions (scallions), chopped
1 red onion, chopped
1 tablespoon extra virgin olive oil
1 tablespoon apple cider vinegar
1 tablespoon lemon juice
125 g (4¹/₂ oz/1 cup) slivered almonds

Cut the broccoli into florets, then steam or blanch the florets until crispy-tender. Rinse under cold running water to stop the cooking process, then set aside to cool.

Meanwhile, preheat the grill (broiler) to medium–high. Put the bacon on a baking tray, then place the tray 8–10 cm (3¹/₄–4 inches) below the grill. Cook the bacon for a few minutes, until it becomes crispy. Leave the bacon to cool, then cut or break it into smaller pieces.

Put the bacon and broccoli in a salad bowl with the spring onion and red onion.

Combine the olive oil, vinegar and lemon juice in a small jar and season with sea salt and freshly ground black pepper. Screw the lid on tightly and shake well. Pour the dressing over the salad, add the almonds and toss gently.

Cover and chill in the refrigerator until ready to serve. Just before serving, toss the almonds through the salad for extra crunch.

Serves 4

Stacked prawn & avocado salad

Prawns and avocado dance so well together, just like Ginger Rogers and Fred Astaire. The perfect partnership transforms this salad into something spectacular.

12 cos (romaine) lettuce leaves

2 avocados, sliced

1 Lebanese (short) cucumber,
   thinly sliced

150 g (5½ oz/1 cup) vine-ripened cherry
   tomatoes, halved

¼ cup mint leaves

1 red onion, thinly sliced

16 cooked prawns (shrimp), peeled

2 tablespoons Lee's Jam Jar Dressing
   (see page 178)

Arrange three lettuce leaves on each of four plates. Stack a quarter of the avocado, cucumber, tomatoes, mint and onion on each.

Arrange four prawns on top of each, drizzle with the dressing and serve.

Serves 4

 Health benefits An exceedingly good source of protein and omega-3 fatty acids, prawns also contain high levels of vitamin B12 — an important vitamin for those with digestive difficulties, as it is essential for making red blood cells (helping protect against anaemia) and nerve cells. Prawns also contain immune system boosters such as zinc, phosphorus, potassium and selenium, as well as iron, calcium and magnesium. Stack 'em high.

Wheat-free tabouleh

If you're on a wheat-free diet and still want to eat tabouleh, quinoa is a flawless substitute, with a textbook consistency and texture. You can throw this heavenly Middle Eastern salad together in 20 minutes, and serve it straightaway or chill to feast on later. A great way to dish it up is in iceberg lettuce cups, drizzled with Lee's Jam Jar Dressing (page 178). It will literally make you stop mid-conversation.

70 g (2½ oz/⅓ cup) quinoa, rinsed
80 g (2¾ oz/2½ cups) flat-leaf (Italian) parsley, chopped
1 handful mint, chopped
2 garlic cloves, crushed
½ teaspoon sea salt
80 ml (2½ fl oz/⅓ cup) lemon juice
2 tablespoons extra virgin olive oil
1 Lebanese (short) cucumber, diced
4 vine-ripened tomatoes, diced
3 spring onions (scallions), sliced
6–8 iceberg lettuce cups, to serve

Cook the quinoa in a saucepan of simmering water until tender, about 15 minutes. Drain and set aside to cool.

In a bowl, combine the parsley, mint, garlic, salt, lemon juice, olive oil, cucumber, tomatoes and spring onion. Season well with freshly ground black pepper.

Add the quinoa and mix thoroughly. Divide among the lettuce cups and serve.

Serves 6–8

 Health benefits Quinoa is a highly nutritious food that originated in South America, where it was considered 'the gold of the Incas'. If you're looking to substitute grains in recipes, quinoa is the perfect choice. It has high levels of amino acids and protein and is a good source of iron, calcium, copper and potassium. The riboflavin present in quinoa reduces the frequency of migraine attacks by relaxing the blood vessels, reducing constriction and easing tension. It's a wonderful food to help prevent conditions such as type 2 diabetes, childhood asthma, heart diseases and gallstones.

Rocket, spinach & tuna salad

This super-healthy salad, packed with protein and luscious vegetables, is a perfect make-ahead dish for lunchboxes or lunch on the run. You'll be amazed at how quick and simple it is to toss together. A year-round palate pleaser, the combination of peppery rocket, juicy tomatoes and creamy avocado gives a kaleidoscope of peppery, sweet, tangy and nutty flavours, from the first to last bite. It's worth buying good-quality canned tuna, rather than the varieties with blended oils. The blended-oil varieties are okay for cats — but for humans, not so much.

185 g (6½ oz) tin tuna in spring water, drained
1 red onion, sliced
2 roma (plum) tomatoes, sliced
1 Lebanese (short) cucumber, thinly sliced
½ avocado, diced
1 handful baby English spinach leaves
1 handful rocket (arugula)
1 tablespoon extra virgin olive oil
1 garlic clove, crushed
1 tablespoon lemon juice
a sprinkling of pepitas (pumpkin seeds), to serve

Break the tuna up into large bite-sized pieces and place in a salad bowl. Add the onion, tomatoes, cucumber, avocado, spinach and rocket and toss gently.

Combine the olive oil, garlic and lemon juice in a small bowl. Drizzle over the salad, sprinkle the pepitas on top and enjoy.

Serves 2

Crunchy Asian slaw

Perfect as a casual side dish or as a topping for burgers, this salad also works as a light meal in its own right. You can have lots of fun with it by adding other vegetables, such as snow peas (mangetout) or bean sprouts. Sesame oil enhances its intensity and gives it more of a smoky flavour.

1 carrot, peeled
1/2 red capsicum (pepper)
1/2 yellow capsicum (pepper)
3 spring onions (scallions)
150 g (5 1/2 oz/2 cups) finely shredded
   green cabbage
150 g (5 1/2 oz/2 cups) finely shredded
   red cabbage
2 teaspoons toasted sesame seeds

Dressing

1 small garlic clove, crushed
2–3 cm (3/4–1 1/4 inch) knob of fresh ginger,
   peeled and grated
2 tablespoons apple cider vinegar
3 tablespoons almond butter
2 tablespoons wheat-free tamari
1/2 teaspoon sesame oil
3 tablespoons lemon juice
5 drops liquid stevia

Julienne the carrot, capsicums and spring onions and place in a salad bowl. Add the cabbage.

Whisk all the dressing ingredients together in a bowl and add sea salt and freshly ground black pepper to taste.

Pour the dressing over the salad, sprinkle with the sesame seeds and toss well. This salad is lovely served slightly chilled.

Serves 4

Antioxidant salad

Eating a diet bursting with antioxidant-rich foods — such as brightly coloured fruits, vegetables and wholefoods — has been linked to a reduced risk of cardiovascular disease. If you're looking for a way to add more antioxidants to your diet, this delicious salad with its full palate of sweet and tangy flavours will have you living the dream. Use the freshest bounty of in-season vegetables for the best results.

6 vine-ripened tomatoes
1 red onion
1 red capsicum (pepper)
1 yellow capsicum (pepper)
1 bunch basil (about 100 g/3½ oz), leaves
1 small handful radicchio leaves, chopped
1 tablespoon chopped parsley
1 tablespoon dried goji berries (optional)
2 teaspoons lime juice
1 tablespoon lemon juice
1 tablespoon extra virgin olive oil

Dice the tomatoes, onion and capsicums and place in a salad bowl. Add the basil leaves, radicchio, parsley and goji berries, if using.

Put the lime juice, lemon juice and olive oil in a small jar and season with sea salt and freshly ground black pepper. Screw the lid on tightly and shake well.

Drizzle the dressing over the salad, toss lightly and serve.

Serves 2

Cucumber side-kick salad

2 Lebanese (short) cucumbers
1 small onion
2 garlic cloves, crushed
2 tablespoons lemon juice
1 tablespoon extra virgin olive oil
1 tablespoon chopped oregano
1 tablespoon chopped mint

Thinly slice the cucumbers and place in a salad bowl. Halve, then thinly slice the onion and add to the bowl.

Put the garlic, lemon juice and olive oil in a small jar and season with sea salt and freshly ground black pepper. Screw the lid on tightly and shake well.

Drizzle the dressing over the salad, then sprinkle the herbs over the top. Cover with plastic wrap and chill before serving.

Serves 2

lunch

Caramelised onion & rosemary frittata

Frittatas are a fantastic light food option for any time of the day, or a quick and satisfying meal on the hop. They are one of the most versatile dishes around as lots of different vegetables or herbs can be added, depending on your mood or the contents of your fridge. This frittata is something really special — aromatic and delicious from the first bite. You'll need a large, non-stick ovenproof frying pan; cast iron is a good option. Enjoy the frittata fresh out of the oven, or serve with a crunchy green leaf salad simply dressed with lemon juice and extra virgin olive oil.

2¹⁄₂ tablespoons extra virgin olive oil
3 large onions, sliced
1 tablespoon rosemary leaves, chopped
8 organic eggs

Heat 2 tablespoons of the olive oil in a medium frying pan. Sauté the onion and rosemary over low heat until the onion is sweet and browned, about 8–10 minutes.

Whisk the eggs lightly in a bowl, then season with sea salt and freshly ground black pepper. Scrape the caramelised onion into the bowl and stir to combine.

Wipe the frying pan clean with a paper towel, add the remaining olive oil and place over very low heat. Pour the egg and onion mixture back into the pan and cook for about 8 minutes, or until the eggs are no longer runny.

For a puffy top, place the frittata under a preheated grill (broiler) for a few minutes, until it is puffed, golden and crisp.

To serve, gently slide a spatula underneath the frittata to loosen it, then turn it out onto a warm plate. Cut into slices and enjoy.

Serves 4

 Health benefits Eggs are a wonderful source of high-quality protein and amino acids, which are essential for a healthy body. Eggs also contain choline, an anti-inflammatory that is particularly important for brain function and cardiovascular health; vitamin E, important for protecting cells against free radical damage; zinc, which is vital for a healthy immune system; and selenium, an important antioxidant that helps prevent blood clots, strokes and heart attacks.

Pizza with tomato, rocket, olives & basil

There are certain times when you just need to eat pizza. Just because you're gluten free, doesn't mean you have to go without. This traditional-tasting pizza is more like the real thing than those store-bought varieties that taste like soggy cardboard with runny tomato sauce and rubbery processed cheese. This homemade version, on the other hand, tastes positively gourmet. Utterly supreme. Scatter it with your favourite toppings and enjoy.

Pizza base

180 g (6 oz/1¾ cups) finely ground
   almond meal

2 organic eggs, beaten

2 tablespoons extra virgin olive oil

2 tablespoons nutritional yeast flakes

1 teaspoon finely chopped oregano or basil

2 garlic cloves, crushed

¼ teaspoon sea salt

1 teaspoon apple cider vinegar

extra almond meal, for rolling the dough

Topping

2 tablespoons sugar-free tomato paste
   (concentrated purée)

75 g (2½ oz/½ cup) sun-dried tomatoes
   or 105 g (3½ oz/½ cup) oven-roasted
   tomatoes, sliced

10 pitted olives, halved

6 anchovy fillets, cut into thin strips
   (optional)

1 tablespoon nutritional yeast flakes

55 g (2 oz/1½ cups) rocket (arugula)

1 cup basil leaves

Preheat the oven to 220°C (425°F/Gas 7) and lightly grease a pizza pan or large baking tray.

To make the pizza base, put the almond meal in a large bowl, add all the other ingredients and mix until you have a loose dough. If the dough feels wet, add a bit more almond meal and work it in with your hands until smooth. Shape the dough into a ball.

Cut the dough in half. Roll each portion out between two sheets of baking paper to make two thin circles about 20 cm (6 inches) in diameter, rolling from the inside of each circle outwards in a clockwise motion. Add more almond meal if the dough becomes too sticky. Place the two pizza bases side by side on the prepared pizza pan/baking tray and bake in the oven for 10 minutes.

Remove the pizza bases from the oven and spread with the tomato paste, leaving a 5 mm (¼ inch) border of dough uncovered. Scatter the tomatoes, olives and anchovies, if using, over the top. Sprinkle with the yeast flakes.

Return the pizzas to the oven for another 7–10 minutes, or until glistening and crispy. Scatter the rocket and basil over each one and they are ready!

Makes 2 small pizzas

Salmon & turnip patties

Turnips are the world's most overcooked — oops, overlooked — vegetable. Many people perceive them as tasting a bit, well, blah, because of their nondescript flavour. In the world of patties, turnips finally get their chance to shine. Delicious and satisfying, these salmon patties with zucchini and lemon taste great and not at all turnipy. The turnip just gives them extra staying power and bulk so they don't fall apart when you cook them, and the lemon zest imparts a flavour punch. Enjoy the patties fresh out of the pan with healthy fries and a zingy salad or refrigerate them and use them for a healthy lunchbox treat.

2 zucchini (courgettes), grated

1 large turnip, peeled and grated

415 g (14¾ oz) tin pink salmon (no additives), well drained, then roughly broken up

1 teaspoon finely grated lemon zest

2 organic eggs, beaten

extra virgin olive oil, for pan-frying

a few parsley sprigs, to garnish

Mayonnaise (see page 179), to serve

Squeeze the excess water out of the grated zucchini and turnip to ensure the patties will be dry and won't fall apart.

Place the grated zucchini and turnip in a bowl with the salmon, lemon zest and eggs. Season well with sea salt and freshly ground black pepper and mix together well. Divide the mixture into six portions and shape each one into a patty.

Heat a little olive oil in a frying pan and fry half the patties over medium heat until lightly browned and cooked through, about 5 minutes on each side. Remove the patties from the pan and keep warm while cooking the remaining patties.

Serve the patties warm, garnished with parsley sprigs and with a dollop of mayonnaise.

Makes 6

Autumn braised vegetables

I'm passionate about simple food, and there's nothing quicker and easier to have midweek when your energy is flagging than a fill of vegetables. Cook up these vegies the night before and take them with you to work — they taste even better the second day. These nutrient-rich, lively vegetables and good fats will pick you up and provide you with a burst of energy. The tahini adds a rich, nutty flavour and thickens the texture. You can swap the coconut oil for sesame oil and add Asian greens such as bok choy.

1 red onion
1 yellow capsicum (pepper)
1 red capsicum (pepper)
100 g (3½ oz) daikon
1 tablespoon coconut oil
2 garlic cloves, crushed
2–3 cm (¾–1¼ inch) knob of fresh ginger, peeled and grated
100 g (3½ oz/2½ cups) torn English spinach leaves
1 small head of broccoli, cut into florets
¼ small cabbage, roughly chopped
125 g (4½ oz/1 cup) green beans, topped and tailed, then sliced in half on the diagonal
1 tablespoon tahini
2 tablespoons wheat-free tamari (optional)
basil leaves, to garnish

Cut the onion and capsicums lengthways into strips and set aside. Peel the daikon, then cut into chip-sized lengths and set aside.

Heat the coconut oil in a very large frying pan over medium–high heat. Add the onion, capsicum, garlic and ginger and stir around for a minute or two until fragrant, but do not allow to burn.

Add the daikon, spinach, broccoli, cabbage and beans and turn the heat down to medium. Cook, stirring, for 5 minutes.

Reduce the heat to low and stir in the tahini and tamari. Cover and cook for 10 minutes. Top with the basil and serve immediately.

Serves 2

Crispy baked herb-encrusted salmon

Brimming with heart-healthy omega-3 oils, these salmon fillets are deliciously dressed up with chopped fresh herbs to create a crunchy and flavoursome crust. Serve up this superfood with bright-green wilted spinach and lemon wedges for the perfect lunchtime delight.

1 tablespoon lemon juice
2 garlic cloves, crushed
2–3 cm (3/4–11/4 inch) knob of fresh ginger, peeled and grated
1 1/2 tablespoons chopped dill
2 teaspoons coconut oil
2 salmon fillets, skin on
lemon wedges, to serve

Preheat the oven to 220°C (425°F/Gas 7). Mix the lemon juice, garlic, ginger and dill together in a small bowl and season with sea salt and freshly ground black pepper.

Pour the coconut oil into a baking dish and place the salmon fillets on top, skin side up. Pour the lemon juice mixture over the salmon. Bake for 15–20 minutes, or until the salmon is cooked through but still moist.

Serve the salmon with lemon wedges. Wilted English spinach is a perfect accompaniment.

Serves 2

Zucchini & celery nut loaf

The first nut loaf I ever made was a disaster. Too squidgy, gooey and tasteless on the inside, and on the outside over-crunchy, like something from the floor of an exotic bird's cage. As I dolloped the goop embarrassingly onto waiting plates I knew everyone was being polite when they said they enjoyed it. Enhanced with herbs, this rustic new recipe will not disappoint — in fact, it's one of my favourite dishes to make for a lazy Sunday lunch.

80 ml (2¹/₂ fl oz/¹/₃ cup) extra virgin
  olive oil
1 onion, finely chopped
2 garlic cloves, crushed
2 celery stalks, diced
1 tablespoon finely chopped mixed herbs
1 teaspoon ground cumin
150 g (5¹/₂ oz/1¹/₂ cups) almond meal
¹/₂ teaspoon stevia powder
¹/₂ teaspoon sea salt
¹/₂ teaspoon gluten-free baking powder
1 organic egg, lightly beaten
2 tablespoons Silky Smooth Almond Milk
  (see page 38)
3 zucchini (courgettes), grated and
  squeezed dry
185 g (6¹/₂ oz/1¹/₂ cups) chopped mixed
  walnuts, brazil nuts and raw cashews
2 teaspoons finely grated lemon zest
1 tablespoon sugar-free tomato paste
  (concentrated purée)
1 tablespoon wheat-free tamari (optional)

Preheat the oven to 160°C (315°F/Gas 2–3). Grease a 21 x 11 cm (8¹/₄ x 4¹/₄ inch) loaf (bar) tin.

Heat half the olive oil in a heavy-based frying pan over medium heat. Add the onion, garlic, celery, herbs and cumin and cook, stirring often, until the onion is translucent. Transfer to a large bowl.

Stir in the almond meal, stevia, salt and baking powder. Add the remaining olive oil and the remaining ingredients and mix well. Spoon the mixture into the prepared tin and level the surface.

Bake for 50–60 minutes, or until crispy and browned on top and set in the middle. Leave to cool for 10 minutes in the tin to allow the loaf to firm up, then turn out onto a rack to cool completely. Carve into slices to serve.

This nut loaf is really good the next day, and will keep well for 4 days in the fridge in an airtight container, or firmly wrapped in foil.

Makes 1 loaf

Light & puffy crustless quiche

Sometimes the greatest excitement in life comes from the simplest of things. Crustless quiche takes the headache out of having to make pastry if you've got other things to do. There's absolutely nothing complicated about this variation on the traditional recipe. Experiment by using different vegetables in this quiche; you can also throw in a handful of cooked sliced organic meat such as chicken or turkey if you have some on hand.

8 organic eggs
125 ml (4 fl oz/½ cup) Silky Smooth
    Almond Milk (see page 38)
½ teaspoon sea salt
2 tablespoons nutritional yeast flakes
    (optional)
1½ cups sautéed chopped mixed
    vegetables, such as onion, garlic,
    English spinach, zucchini (courgette),
    red capsicum (pepper), tomato and
    rocket (arugula)
75 g (2½ oz/½ cup) sautéed chopped
    bacon (nitrate and sugar free), optional

Preheat the oven to 180°C (350°F/Gas 4) and grease a 22 cm (8½ inch) diameter pie dish.

Whisk the eggs well in a large bowl, then whisk in the almond milk, salt and yeast flakes, if using. Scatter the vegetables and bacon in the pie dish and pour the egg mixture over the top.

Bake for 25–30 minutes, or until the quiche is set in the middle and the top is puffy and slightly browned.

Enjoy warm or at room temperature.

Serves 4

Quinoa risotto with tomato, basil, lemon & hazelnuts

750 ml (26 fl oz/3 cups) additive-free
   vegetable stock or filtered water
2–3 tablespoons extra virgin olive oil
1 onion, chopped
3 garlic cloves, crushed
100 g (3½ oz) yellow zucchini
   (courgette), chopped
65 g (2¼ oz/½ cup) hazelnuts, roughly
   crushed (save a few whole nuts for
   garnishing)
200 g (7 oz/1 cup) quinoa, rinsed
400 g (14 oz) tin chopped tomatoes
   (sugar and additive free)
45 g (1½ oz/1 cup) baby English spinach
   leaves, washed
1 tablespoon chopped mixed rosemary,
   oregano and thyme
¼ cup torn basil leaves, plus extra
   to garnish
1 tablespoon apple cider vinegar
½ teaspoon finely grated lemon zest
2 tablespoons lemon juice
⅛ teaspoon ground nutmeg
½ teaspoon sea salt
4 tablespoons nutritional yeast flakes

Pour the stock or water into a saucepan and heat to just below boiling. Leave it sitting on the heat, maintaining the temperature.

Heat the olive oil in a large saucepan and sauté the onion and garlic over medium heat for 3 minutes, or until translucent, stirring often. Add the zucchini and hazelnuts and cook for a few minutes, until slightly browned.

Push the mixture to the side of the pan, then add the quinoa and fry, stirring, for 2–3 minutes, or until slightly toasted.

Mix everything in the pan together, turn up the heat and stir in enough of the hot stock or water to just cover the quinoa. Cook, stirring often, until all the liquid has been absorbed. Stir in another 250 ml (9 fl oz/1 cup) of hot stock and cook until it has been absorbed, then continue in this way, letting each addition of stock be absorbed before adding the next.

Add all the remaining ingredients ,except the yeast flakes. Cook for 8–10 minutes, until the quinoa is tender but still slightly *al dente*.

Remove from the heat, season with freshly ground black pepper and stir the yeast flakes through. Serve warm, garnished with reserved hazelnuts and extra basil leaves.

Serves 4

Fabulous fishy burgers

Got a hankering for a burger and chips? Try this healthy match made in heaven. When it comes to fish burgers, sometimes less is more: the trick with this burger is to keep it simple. Before you know it, this dish will be a repeat performer on your weekly lunch menu. Serve it with Crunchy Daikon Chips (see page 151).

2 tablespoons Mayonnaise (see page 179)
4 slices gluten-free bread, toasted or
   Spinach Toast (see page 170)
2–4 lettuce leaves
1/2 Lebanese (short) cucumber, sliced
1/2 avocado, sliced
8 cherry tomatoes, halved
1 tablespoon extra virgin olive oil
4 garlic cloves, thinly sliced
2 (about 200 g/7 oz each) skinless white
   fish fillets, of medium thickness
1 lime, quartered

Spread the mayonnaise over two slices of the toasted bread. Arrange the lettuce leaves, cucumber, avocado and tomatoes on top.

Heat the olive oil in a frying pan over medium–low heat and briefly fry the garlic slices until golden. Remove from the pan and set aside.

Add the fish fillets to the pan and fry until cooked through, about 2–3 minutes on each side. Remove from the pan and place a fillet on top of each open burger.

Sprinkle the fish with sea salt and freshly ground black pepper, then scatter the garlic slices over the top. Place the remaining slices of toasted bread on each burger. Serve immediately with the lime quarters.

Serves 2

dinner

Maharajah Indian stuffed capsicums

If you have leftover cooked quinoa, this is a great way to use it up. You'll need about 1 cup of cooked quinoa.

2 red capsicums (peppers)
2 yellow capsicums (peppers)
2 tablespoons coconut oil
1 onion, finely chopped
2 garlic cloves, crushed
1 teaspoon cumin seeds
1/2 teaspoon cayenne pepper
1 red chilli, seeded and finely
    chopped (optional)
2 teaspoons ground coriander
1 teaspoon grated fresh ginger
400 g (14 oz) minced (ground)
    organic beef
400 g (14 oz) tin chopped tomatoes
    (sugar and additive free)
1/2 teaspoon sea salt
70 g (2 1/2 oz/1 cup) quinoa, rinsed
basil leaves, to garnish

Preheat the oven to 220°C (425°F/Gas 7). Bring a large saucepan of filtered water to the boil. Cut off the tops of the capsicums and remove the seeds and membranes. Drop the capsicum shells into the water and simmer for 3–4 minutes — you may need to do this in two batches, depending on the size of your saucepan. Carefully remove the capsicums with a slotted spoon and drain well.

Heat the coconut oil in a frying pan and sauté the onion and garlic over medium heat until golden, 6–8 minutes. Add the cumin seeds to one side of the pan and toast them until they pop, then stir them in to the onion with the cayenne pepper, chilli (if using), coriander and ginger. Add the beef, tomatoes and salt and cook for 20 minutes, stirring often to break up any lumps in the meat.

Meanwhile, cook the quinoa in a saucepan of simmering water until tender, about 15 minutes. Drain the quinoa, then stir it through the beef mixture.

Divide the mixture among the capsicums, filling them loosely. Sit them in a baking tin and loosely cover the tin with foil. Bake for 15 minutes, then remove the foil. Continue baking until the capsicums start to blister, another 10–15 minutes.

Sprinkle the tops with basil and serve.

Serves 2

Lamburgers with rosemary

The best thing about these burgers is that you can prepare them in the morning, or the day before, and have them ready to go at a moment's notice, especially if you don't feel like cooking after a busy day at work. Crunchy Daikon Chips (page 151) are the perfect partner to these super-easy crowd pleasers.

500 g (1 lb 2 oz) minced (ground) lamb,
    organic if possible
1/2 onion, finely chopped
2 garlic cloves, crushed
1 organic egg, lightly beaten
1 teaspoon finely chopped rosemary leaves
1 tablespoon extra virgin olive oil
8 slices Super Seeded Bread (see page 175),
    or other gluten-free bread
1 Lebanese (short) cucumber, thinly sliced
2 tomatoes, sliced
1 avocado, sliced
2 tablespoons Aïoli (page 179)

Combine the lamb, onion, garlic, egg and rosemary in a bowl and season well with sea salt and freshly ground black pepper. Divide the mixture into four equal portions, then shape each one into a patty using your hands.

Heat the olive oil in a frying pan and add the patties. Cook over medium heat for about 6 minutes on each side, or until crusty brown on the outside and cooked through.

Meanwhile, toast the bread.

Top four of the bread slices with cucumber, tomato and avocado. Place a patty on each with a dollop aïoli. Crown them with the remaining toasts and serve straight away.

Serves 4

Slow-cooked Greek lamb

For a taste of the Mediterranean, there's nothing more special than this succulent lamb, all sweet and tender and melt-in-the-mouth.

3 tablespoons extra virgin olive oil
4 garlic cloves, crushed
4 tablespoons lemon juice
1 tablespoon dried oregano
1.8–2 kg (4–4 lb 8 oz) leg of lamb,
   organic if possible
750 ml (26 fl oz/3 cups) filtered water,
   approximately
1–2 lemon wedges
2 tablespoons chopped parsley

Preheat the oven to 160°C (315°F/Gas 2–3). Mix 2 tablespoons of the olive oil, garlic, lemon juice and oregano together in a small bowl, and season well with sea salt and freshly ground black pepper. Rub the garlic mixture all over the lamb.

Place the lamb on a rack in a roasting tin. Pour filtered water into the tin to a depth of about 2 cm (3/4 inch). Bake the lamb for 5 hours, basting every hour with the pan juices. Remove the lamb from the oven and let it rest for 15 minutes.

To serve, place the whole leg on a warm platter in the centre of the table. Squeeze the juice from the lemon wedges over the lamb, then drizzle with the remaining extra virgin olive oil. Flake the meat off the bone with a fork, sprinkle with a little sea salt and freshly ground black pepper, scatter the parsley over and serve.

Serves 4–6

Garlic, lemon & rosemary chicken

6 garlic cloves

2 rosemary bunches (each bunch about
   20 g/¾ oz)

1.6 kg (3 lb 8 oz) organic chicken

2 tablespoons extra virgin olive oil

2 tablespoons lemon juice

1 lemon, sliced

3 daikon

Preheat the oven to 220°C (425°F/Gas 7). Peel and slice two of the garlic cloves, leaving the others whole and unpeeled. Pick the sprigs from the rosemary bunches.

Place the chicken in a roasting tin and drizzle the olive oil and lemon juice over the skin. Sprinkle the chicken well with sea salt and freshly ground black pepper. Make small nicks in the skin of the chicken using a sharp knife, then tuck the sliced garlic into them. Push most of the rosemary sprigs and lemon slices into the cavity of the chicken, then scatter the rest over the top. Add the unpeeled garlic cloves to the roasting tin.

Peel the daikon. Cut them lengthways into 1–2 cm (½–¾ inch) thick slices, then chop these into chips. Scatter the daikon around the chicken in the tin.

Roast the chicken for 1 hour 20 minutes, basting periodically with the pan juices.

Remove the chicken and daikon chips from the oven, cover loosely with foil and leave to rest for 10 minutes.

Carve the chicken and serve with the roasted garlic cloves, which release a sweet and mushy flesh when squeezed out of their skins and daikon chips.

Cauliflower Mash (page 142) and steamed broccoli are also excellent accompaniments to this dish.

Serves 4

Steamed fish with snow pea, minted fennel & onion salad

With its many virtuous health properties, steamed fish is an ideal dinner choice if you're trying to steer away from eating too much red meat. Choose whichever fish you prefer and pair it with this gorgeous salad. Try the salad as an accompaniment to other dishes, or as part of a summer picnic.

2 white fish fillets, about 200 g (7 oz) each

1 handful pine nuts, to serve (optional)

Snow pea, minted fennel & onion salad

2 baby fennel bulbs, thinly sliced

150 g (5½ oz) snow peas (mangetout), trimmed

1 handful mint leaves

½ red onion, thinly sliced

Dressing

2 tablespoons lemon juice

3 tablespoons extra virgin olive oil

2 garlic cloves, crushed

4 drops liquid stevia

Bring a saucepan of water to a simmer. Line a metal or bamboo steamer with baking paper to prevent sticking, then place the fish on top. Cover the steamer and place over the saucepan of simmering water. Steam the fish until it becomes opaque — about 6–10 minutes, depending on the type of fish and its thickness.

Meanwhile, put the salad ingredients in a salad bowl. Whisk the dressing ingredients in a small bowl and season to taste with sea salt and freshly ground black pepper.

Just before serving, drizzle the dressing over the salad and toss lightly. Pile the salad onto two serving plates, then top each salad with a fish fillet. Sprinkle with the pine nuts, if using, and serve.

Serves 2

Pasta puttanesca

Gluten-free pasta is a fabulous base for this rich, flavoursome sauce. Alternatively, you can create vegetable pasta with a spiraliser. Zucchini noodles ('zoodles') work well and are beautiful when lightly steamed or sautéed in olive oil. You can knock up any type of 'pasta' from raw vegetables — from wide ribbon pappardelle to angel hair — and you can even produce paper-thin slices that can be used to make ravioli. When I started eating gluten-free I felt I was missing out on pasta, but the spiraliser has since opened up a whole new world of pasta ideas.

1 tablespoon extra virgin olive oil

40 g (1½ oz/¼ cup) pine nuts

2 garlic cloves, crushed

1 onion, chopped

4 anchovies, chopped

6 vine-ripened tomatoes, peeled and chopped, or a 400 g (14 oz) tin chopped tomatoes (sugar and additive free)

2 tablespoons sugar-free tomato paste (concentrated purée)

60 g (2¼ oz/½ cup) black olives, chopped

2 tablespoons capers, rinsed

1 handful mixed herbs, such as basil or rosemary, thyme and oregano, chopped

cooked gluten-free pasta, or lightly steamed zucchini 'pasta', to serve

sprigs of thyme, to garnish

Heat the olive oil in a frying pan. Sauté the pine nuts, garlic and onion over medium heat until browned, about 4–5 minutes.

Add the anchovies, tomatoes and tomato paste and cook over medium heat for 10 minutes, stirring often. Stir in the olives, capers, herbs and sea salt to taste and simmer for 5 minutes.

Serve the sauce over cooked gluten-free pasta or lightly steamed zucchini 'pasta'. Garnish with sprigs of thyme.

Serves 2

Supercharged tip I bought my spiraliser online — you should be able to pick one up quite cheaply. When using a spiraliser, ensure your vegetables are straight and not too bent, otherwise they won't fit into the ends of the spiraliser and will topple over as you are spinning the top wheel. Using an even pressure will give you the best results.

Slow-cooked lamb shanks with rosemary & lemon

Lamb shanks are fabulous in winter, and there's no slaving over a hotpot with this hearty creation. It really couldn't be easier to make: pop it on in the morning and come home to an intensely flavoursome and fulfilling meal, the succulent slow-cooked meat just falling off the bone. You can also throw in some seasonal vegetables if you have some. Partner it with some Crunchy Daikon Chips (see page 151) and Cauliflower Mash (see page 142) and it's a win–win situation.

4 lamb shanks, organic if possible
2 garlic cloves, crushed
1 small handful rosemary sprigs
1 tablespoon extra virgin olive oil
1 carrot, diced
1 celery stalk, diced
1 onion, diced
250 ml (9 fl oz/1 cup) Homemade
   Chicken Stock (see page 183)
2 tablespoons lemon juice
1 teaspoon sea salt

Put the lamb shanks in a slow cooker and add the garlic, rosemary and olive oil. Turn the shanks over a few times to coat them with the oil. Add the remaining ingredients and give a few good grinds of black pepper.

Set the cooker on low and leave to cook for 8 hours. The shanks can also be cooked in a 100°C (200°F/Gas 1/2) oven for 6 hours.

When you get home, change the heat setting to 'keep warm' until you are ready to eat.

Transfer the shanks to a warmed wide serving bowl and spoon the sauce over the top. Serve with your favourite accompaniments.

Serves 4

Bollywood Bombay chicken curry

Chicken thighs are best suited to this curry. They hold their moisture well and are tender and succulent to the bite.

1¹/₂ tablespoons coconut oil

4 onions, thinly sliced

4 garlic cloves, crushed

1 tablespoon grated fresh ginger

1 tablespoon cumin seeds

2 teaspoons ground coriander

750 g (1 lb 10 oz) organic chicken
  thigh fillets, diced

400 ml (14 fl oz) Homemade Coconut
  Milk (see page 44)

1 large tomato, diced

2 tablespoons lemon juice

1 teaspoon ground turmeric

1 teaspoon sea salt

Heat half the coconut oil in a large saucepan over medium heat. Add the onion, garlic and ginger and sauté until browned, about 6–8 minutes.

Slide the onion mixture to one side of the pan. To the other side add the remaining coconut oil, cumin seeds and coriander and toast them until they are aromatic. Mix the spices through the onion mixture, then add the remaining ingredients and a few grinds of black pepper.

Stir well, then cover and reduce the heat to low. Simmer for about 30 minutes, or until the chicken is tender and the sauce is thick.

This curry is delicious with steamed brown rice.

Serves 3

Shepherd's pie with cauliflower mash

A new take on a golden oldie, this is a firm favourite in our family. You can bake individual pies for lunch — a distinct bonus if you're eating alone — and serve with a leafy salad. Don't be afraid to pep up the pie with your favourite seasoning or mixed herbs. The delicious cauliflower mash can be used instead of potato mash in so many dishes that you'll never feel you're missing out on mash again. As a side dish, the mash makes enough for 3–4 servings.

2 tablespoons extra virgin olive oil

1 large onion, chopped

2 garlic cloves, crushed

1 celery stalk, chopped

500 g (1 lb 2 oz) lean minced (ground) lamb, organic if possible

2 anchovies, chopped

1/2 x 400 g (14 oz) tin chopped tomatoes (sugar and additive free)

125 ml (4 fl oz/1/2 cup) tomato passata (puréed tomato)

1 teaspoon sea salt

1 teaspoon freshly ground black pepper

1/4 teaspoon liquid stevia (optional)

Cauliflower mash

1 cauliflower, cut into florets

1 tablespoon extra virgin olive oil, or organic butter (if tolerated)

1 tablespoon nutritional yeast flakes

Heat the olive oil in a large frying pan. Add the onion, garlic and celery and sauté over medium–low heat for 8–10 minutes, or until the onion is golden brown. Add the lamb and anchovies and cook for a further 5 minutes, stirring often to break up any lumps in the meat.

Stir in the chopped tomatoes, passata, salt and pepper, then cover and cook over low heat for 20 minutes. If there is excess liquid in the pan, turn the heat up and simmer, uncovered, for a few minutes more. Stir in the stevia, if using.

Meanwhile, preheat the oven to 220°C (425°F/Gas 7) and make the cauliflower mash. Put the florets in a steamer over a saucepan of simmering water and cook, covered, until tender — the florets can be verging on soft, but shouldn't be falling apart. Transfer the cauliflower to a blender or food processor and add the olive oil, yeast flakes, a pinch of sea salt and a few grinds of black pepper. Blend until smooth.

Transfer the cooked lamb mixture to an 18 cm (7 inch) square baking dish and level the surface. Gently spoon the cauliflower mash over the top, scraping a fork across the surface to create little trenches in the mash.

Bake for 20 minutes, or until the mash has a crispy top. Remove the pie from the oven and serve in warmed wide bowls. Fresh minted peas are an excellent accompaniment.

Serves 4

 Health benefits Loaded with folate, cauliflower helps improve cell growth and reproduction and acts as a blood and liver detoxer.

Slow-cooked chicken saag

I'm in love with aromatic curries. This spiffy saag is so simple to make it virtually cooks itself while you're doing the things you need to do. Pop it in the slow cooker in the morning and when you get home, it's there waiting for you — all warm and soothing, like a comfy pair of slippers. Saag is so perfectly delicate in flavour, and this recipe tastes just divine. It's not overpoweringly pungent or super spicy, so there'll be no hurried trips to the vindaloo!

4 bunches (approx 800 g/1 lb 12 oz)
    English spinach
1 tablespoon coconut oil
1 large onion, chopped
3 garlic cloves, crushed
2–3 cm (³/4–1¹/4 inch) knob of fresh
    ginger, peeled and grated
250 ml (9 fl oz/1 cup) Homemade
    Coconut Milk (see page 44)
3 tablespoons red curry paste
    (no additives)
1 teaspoon finely grated lemon zest
1 tablespoon lemon juice
500 g (1 lb 2 oz) organic chicken thigh
    fillets, cut into bite-sized pieces
2 tablespoons chopped coriander
    (cilantro)
cooked brown rice, to serve (optional)
coriander (cilantro) sprigs, to garnish
lime wedges, to serve

Strip the leaves from the spinach stalks and rinse them. Drain and shake the leaves well to get rid of excess water, then finely chop and set aside.

Heat the coconut oil in a large frying pan. Sauté the onion, garlic and ginger over medium–low heat until the onion browns, about 5–6 minutes. Stir in the coconut milk, curry paste, lemon zest and lemon juice.

Add the spinach in batches, using tongs to turn the leaves over to wilt them and make room for the next batch. Stir the chicken and half the coriander through, then season with sea salt.

Transfer the mixture to a slow cooker and set the cooker on low. Cook for 5 hours, or longer if this suits your timing better. This dish can also be cooked in a 100°C (200°F/Gas ¹/2) oven for 5 hours.

Serve the saag on its own or with steamed brown rice, topped with the coriander sprigs and accompanied by lime wedges.

Serves 3

 Health benefits Spinach is a powerful anti-inflammatory food, loaded with calcium, folic acid, vitamins A, C, E and K, zinc, iron, carotenoids and fibre. Its nutrient profile makes it beneficial for a number of vital processes, helping eyesight, the nervous system, cardiovascular disorders, lowering high blood pressure and strengthening muscles.

vegetables

Simple oven-roasted vegetables

For this easy-peasy dish, select enough mixed vegetables to serve four hungry people. Choose from the freshest seasonal vegies you can find — turnip, pumpkin (winter squash), zucchini (courgette), cauliflower, fennel, red and yellow capsicum (pepper), eggplant (aubergine), parsnip and onion are especially good. Also include garlic if you like.

**mixed seasonal vegetables of your
    choice (enough for 4 people)**

Dressing

2 garlic cloves, crushed

1/2 teaspoon dried oregano

1/2 teaspoon dried basil

1/2 teaspoon dried rosemary

3 tablespoons extra virgin olive oil

1 tablespoon apple cider vinegar

2 tablespoons lemon juice

Preheat the oven to 250°C (500°F/Gas 9). Peel and chop your vegetables into chunks or wedges and place in a large bowl.

Put all the dressing ingredients in a jar. Screw the lid on tightly, shake well, then pour over the vegetables. Toss the vegetables well, making sure they are evenly coated in the dressing.

Spread the vegetables in a large roasting tin and season with sea salt and freshly ground black pepper. Roast for 35–40 minutes, or until the vegetables are tender, browned and crispy, turning and basting them halfway through. Transfer to a warmed platter to serve.

Serves 4

 Supercharged tip If the vegetables are browning too quickly, reduce the oven temperature to 220°C (425°F/Gas 7). Not all vegetables have the same cooking times, so keep checking them and remove any that are fully cooked. Put them back in the oven for the last 5 minutes or so to heat through.

Crunchy daikon chips

These daikon chips have become an institution at home. Once you start making and enjoying them I guarantee you won't even want to go back to conventional potato chips! My husband Sebastian, a recovering carboholic, is completely enamoured by these — what is it with guys and fries? When you bake these chips, the radish taste soon disappears and they brown up beautifully with the addition of sea salt and olive oil. Crunchy turnip chips can be made in the same way. Substitute turnips for the daikon, and oregano for rosemary, and roast for about 40 minutes. Using the big round purple turnips gives the best results, and I size them somewhere between a shoestring chip and a wedge.

4 large daikon
2 tablespoons extra virgin olive oil
1 teaspoon sea salt
1 tablespoon rosemary leaves,
  coarsely chopped

Preheat the oven to 155°C (310°F/Gas 2–3). Peel each daikon and cut them into chips about 5 cm (2 inches) long, and of an even 2–3 cm (3/4–1¼ inch) thickness.

Spread the chips in a single layer on two baking trays. Drizzle the olive oil over and sprinkle with the sea salt and rosemary. Toss to coat evenly.

Roast for 35–40 minutes, or until the chips are golden brown and crunchy, turning them two or three times.

Transfer to a bowl or a platter, sprinkle with freshly ground black pepper and serve at once.

Serves 4

Health Benefits: Daikon also stacks up nutritionally: a natural digestive, it is rich in vitamins A, C and E, making it a very healthy snack option. Turnips are also a fantastic source of vitamin C, calcium and iron — their juice has twice as much vitamin C as orange juice, without all the fructose.

Oven-roasted cauliflower

Main meals feel bare without vegetables, like a keyhole without a key. And the truth is vegetables are the key to a radiant and energetic life. Adding a new array of vegetables to your diet will boost your nutrient levels and keep you feeling fuller for longer. Cauliflower contains vitamin C and folate, which is often recommended for preventing anaemia, and a good roasting really brings out its nutty sweetness. When buying cauliflower, make sure the florets are free of brown spots, which indicate it is past its nutritional peak.

3 tablespoons extra virgin olive oil

2 tablespoons lemon juice

3 garlic cloves, crushed

1/2 teaspoon ground cumin

1 teaspoon ground turmeric

1 cauliflower, cut into florets

1 tablespoon nutritional yeast flakes

3 spring onions (scallions), sliced

3 tablespoons chopped coriander (cilantro)

Preheat the oven to 200°C (400°F/Gas 6). Mix the olive oil, lemon juice, garlic, cumin and turmeric together in a small bowl and add some sea salt and freshly ground black pepper.

Spread the cauliflower florets in a baking dish and pour the dressing over them. Toss well to ensure each floret is evenly coated.

Roast for 40 minutes, or until the cauliflower is golden and crunchy. Sprinkle with the yeast flakes, spring onion and coriander, and serve.

Serves 4

Sautéed green beans with anchovies & egg

2 tablespoons extra virgin olive oil
4 anchovies, finely chopped
1 tablespoon lemon juice
3 tablespoons Homemade Chicken
   Stock (see page 183)
500 g (1 lb 2 oz) green beans,
   topped and tailed
2 organic eggs, hard-boiled, peeled
   and cut in half lengthways

Put the olive oil, anchovies, lemon juice and stock in a small saucepan. Stir over low heat to combine, then keep warm.

Steam the beans until tender-crisp. Drain the beans, then arrange on a serving plate. Drizzle with the anchovy sauce, garnish with the boiled egg halves and serve. This dish is also good at room temperature.

Serves 4

Sautéed greens

Spinach has innate versatility in my kitchen. This verdant leafy green finds its way into omelettes, salads, soups, stir-fries, bread and muffins. This dish is a grounding example of just how much my tastebuds have transformed — I now crave a large bowl of sautéed greens whenever I'm in need of a pick-me-up or iron boost.

2 bunches (approx 400 g/14 oz) English
   spinach
2 tablespoons extra virgin olive oil
3 garlic cloves, sliced
3 tablespoons additive-free vegetable stock
   or filtered water
lemon juice, for drizzling

Strip the spinach leaves from the stalk, rinse them well and shake dry. Chop the leaves roughly.

Heat the olive oil in a wide, heavy-based frying pan over low heat. Add the garlic and fry until golden but not brown, about 4 minutes. Add the spinach and toss it around to coat in the oil for a further 2 minutes.

Pour in the stock and season with sea salt and freshly ground black pepper. Cover and cook over low heat for 10 minutes, turning the spinach with tongs once or twice to cook evenly.

Transfer to a serving dish, drizzle with lemon juice to taste and serve.

Serves 3–4

Green peas with onion & bacon

My friend Emma, who is a great home cook, makes an amazing version of this recipe, adding some crumbled feta cheese to the mix. This dairy-free alternative uses nutritional yeast flakes to add a cheesy, nutty flavour. This fabulously quick side dish goes with just about anything.

2 tablespoons extra virgin olive oil
1 onion, chopped
2 garlic cloves, sliced
4 bacon slices (nitrate and sugar free)
500 g (1 lb 2 oz) frozen peas
2 tablespoons chopped mint, to garnish
1 tablespoon nutritional yeast flakes

Heat half the olive oil in a small frying pan over medium–low heat and fry the onion and garlic until browned, about 4–5 minutes.

Meanwhile, preheat the grill (broiler) to high and grill (broil) the bacon until crisp. Break the bacon up into 8–10 smaller pieces.

Heat the remaining olive oil in a large saucepan over medium heat and cook the peas for 5 minutes, stirring occasionally. Stir in the onion mixture and reduce the heat to low, then cover and cook for 10 minutes.

Scatter the bacon, mint and yeast flakes over the top and serve.

Serves 4

desserts & baked goods

Butternut cookies

These dangerously delicious cookies are a keeper and will elicit a 'wow' reaction from all. It's my dear friend Louise's snack of choice when she comes over for afternoon tea, and I always have a box of these on hand for those special occasions or just in case unexpected visitors drop by. If they're a few days old, you can warm the cookies in the oven for that just-baked flavour.

150 g (5½ oz/1 cup) coconut flour
¼ teaspoon gluten-free baking powder
1½ teaspoons stevia powder, plus extra
   to dust
a pinch of sea salt
200 g (7 oz) cashew butter
4 organic eggs, lightly beaten
2½ teaspoons natural vanilla extract
2 tablespoons coconut oil
2 tablespoons Homemade Coconut
   Milk (see page 44)

Preheat the oven to 175°C (345°F/Gas 4) and grease a baking tray.

In a bowl, mix together the coconut flour, baking powder, stevia and salt.

Warm the cashew butter slightly, then mix it with the eggs, vanilla, coconut oil and coconut milk until smooth. Add to the dry ingredients and mix well to form a dough.

Roll the dough out between two sheets of baking paper to a thickness of 6–8 mm (¼–3/8 inch). Cut out shapes using your favourite cookie cutter and place them on the greased baking tray (these cookies won't spread during baking).

Bake for 20–25 minutes, or until the cookies are crisp and golden. Leave them to cool on the tray a little before transferring to a wire rack to cool completely. Dust with extra stevia if desired. The cookies will keep in an airtight container for several days.

Makes about 24

Banana & coconut muffins

200 g (7 oz/2 cups) almond meal

¼ teaspoon bicarbonate of soda
  (baking soda)

½ teaspoon gluten-free baking powder

1 tablespoon arrowroot (tapioca) flour

3 organic eggs

3 ripe bananas, mashed

3 tablespoons grape seed oil

3 tablespoons Homemade Coconut
  Milk (see page 44)

6 drops liquid stevia

Preheat the oven to 180°C (350°F/Gas 4) and line
a 12-hole standard muffin tin with paper cases.

Put the almond meal, bicarbonate of soda, baking powder
and arrowroot flour in a bowl and stir to combine.

In a separate bowl, use an electric mixer to whisk the eggs
until pale and fluffy, about 1 minute. Stir in the banana,
grape seed oil, coconut milk and stevia. Pour into the dry
ingredients and mix until just combined.

Spoon the batter into the lined muffin holes and bake
for 15 minutes, or until the muffins have set.

Remove the muffins from the tin and leave to cool on a
wire rack. The muffins will keep in an airtight container
for a day or two.

Makes 12

Coconut & almond bliss balls

You can easily make these bliss balls the day before you need them. They will harden when you refrigerate them, so pull them out of the fridge about 30 minutes before you plan to serve them.

50 g (1¾ oz/½ cup) almond meal

30 g (1 oz/½ cup) coconut flakes

40 g (1½ oz/¼ cup) sesame seeds

125 g (4½ oz/1 cup) chopped mixed nuts, such as walnuts, cashews and pistachios

7 tablespoons (170 g/16 oz) almond or cashew butter, softened

3 tablespoons tahini

½ teaspoon natural vanilla extract

8 drops liquid stevia

extra sesame seeds, for coating

extra chopped mixed nuts, for coating

Put the almond meal, coconut flakes, sesame seeds, nuts, nut butter, tahini, vanilla and stevia in a bowl and mix with a wooden spoon until combined.

Using your hands, take scant tablespoonfuls of the mixture and roll each one into a ball. Roll half the balls in the sesame seeds and the other half in the chopped nuts, coating them all over.

Place the balls on a flat tray and refrigerate until party time.

Makes 14–16

 Supercharged tip Coconut is an excellent tonic for clear skin and healthy hair, and a wonderful digestive, too.

Dairy-free coconut, almond & vanilla ice cream

There are few things as irresistible as dreamy, creamy ice cream in summer, and whipping up a luscious home batch is the perfect way to cool down on a sizzling day. With its soft creamy texture and melt-in-the-mouth taste, it's a satisfying and healthy treat. An ice-cream maker will make your dessert smooth and scoopable, but you can make this recipe without one. For a creamier ice cream, add two more egg yolks.

500 ml (17 fl oz/2 cups) cold Silky Smooth Almond Milk (see page 38), plus 80 g (2¾ oz/¾ cup) almond pulp (left over from making the almond milk)

2 teaspoons powdered gelatine

4 organic egg yolks

400 ml (14 fl oz) tin coconut cream

30 g (1 oz/½ cup) coconut flakes

12 drops liquid stevia

2 teaspoons natural vanilla extract

Pour the almond milk into a small saucepan and sprinkle the gelatine over the surface. Leave for a few minutes while the gelatine softens. Put the saucepan over low heat and stir the mixture until the milk has heated and the gelatine has dissolved. Remove from the heat and place the saucepan in a sink of iced water so that the milk can cool to room temperature.

Put the egg yolks in a blender and process until pale, about 1 minute. Add the coconut cream, almond pulp, coconut flakes, stevia, vanilla and a pinch of sea salt and process until well combined. Add the gelatine milk and blend for a few more seconds. Place in the fridge and leave to chill.

Pour the cold mixture into an ice-cream maker and churn following the manufacturer's instructions.

If you don't have an ice-cream maker, pour the mixture into an ice-cream container and place in the freezer. After 1½ hours, mix it up with a stick blender or fork, then return it to the freezer for an hour. Blend the mixture again to break up the ice crystals, as these make the ice cream more icy than creamy. Freeze until required.

The ice cream can be stored in the freezer for up to 2 weeks. It will be quite hard when it comes out of the freezer, so leave it at room temperature to soften for 15 minutes before serving.

To be truly decadent, serve the ice cream garnished with toasted coconut flakes, mint leaves and a cinnamon stick!

Serves 4–6

Spinach toast

These supercharged spinach slices are surprisingly delicious and will win over even the most avowed spinach haters. Top them with lemon-drizzled avocado and fresh tomato sprinkled with Celtic sea salt for an appetising morning or mid-afternoon snack.

2 organic eggs
1.5 kg (3 lb 5 oz) frozen chopped spinach
   (no additives), thawed and drained well
1/4 teaspoon ground nutmeg
2 garlic cloves, crushed
1/4 teaspoon sea salt

Preheat the oven to 200°C (400°F/Gas 6). Grease two shallow baking trays measuring about 18 x 28 cm (7 x 11 1/4 inches) each.

Beat the eggs in a bowl. Add the spinach, nutmeg and garlic and mix together well, then season with the sea salt and some freshly ground black pepper. Transfer the mixture to the prepared baking trays and press it flat with your hand or the back of the spoon.

Bake the spinach mixture for about 30 minutes, or until set. Remove from the oven and allow to cool slightly, then cut each tray of spinach into six slices, using a sharp knife or kitchen scissors.

To serve, toast the spinach slices in a sandwich toaster or under a grill (broiler) until slightly crispy.

If you're not using them straight away, wrap tightly and freeze until ready to use. They can be frozen for up to 3 months. There is no need to thaw them — just unwrap and toast them straight from the freezer.

Makes 12 slices

Almond & zucchini bread

A *seasonal* classic, this moist, luscious, melt-in-the-mouth bread is often completely gobbled up by the family the day it's baked. It's fun to make, too, as you pile hundreds of tiny strands of zucchini goodness into the rich, creamy batter. It all melds together to create a gorgeous combination of textures and flavours. I now use butter in this loaf, but grape seed oil works just as well.

450 g (1 lb) zucchini (courgettes)
1/4 teaspoon sea salt
1/2 teaspoon stevia powder
65 g (21/2 oz/1/2 cup) buckwheat flour
200 g (7 oz/2 cups) almond meal
1/4 teaspoon bicarbonate of soda
   (baking soda)
11/2 teaspoons gluten-free baking powder
1/4 teaspoon ground cinnamon
1/4 teaspoon ground nutmeg
3 organic eggs
125 ml (4 fl oz/1/2 cup) grape seed oil
   or 125 g (41/2 oz) butter, melted
   (if tolerated)
3 tablespoons Homemade Coconut
   Milk (see page 44)
1 teaspoon lemon juice

Preheat the oven to 175°C (345°F/Gas 4). Grease and flour a 20 x 9 cm (8 x 31/2 inch) loaf (bar) tin.

Grate the zucchini and put it in a sieve set over a bowl. (You can hand-grate the zucchini with a microplane grater, or use a food processor with a grating attachment, which will give you perfectly shredded zukes in a quarter of the time.) Mix the salt through and leave for 20 minutes to allow the salt to draw out excess liquid.

Put the stevia, buckwheat flour, almond meal, bicarbonate of soda, baking powder, cinnamon and nutmeg in a bowl and stir well to combine.

In a separate bowl, whisk the eggs with an electric mixer until pale and fluffy, about 11/2 minutes. Add the grape seed oil, coconut milk and lemon juice and beat well to combine, then stir the mixture into the dry ingredients.

Squeeze the last of the moisture from the zucchini, then stir it into the bread mixture. Spoon into the prepared tin and level the surface with the back of a spoon dipped in cold water.

Bake the loaf on the middle rack of the oven for about 45 minutes, or until a skewer inserted in the centre comes out clean. Turn out onto a wire rack to cool, then enjoy!

The bread will keep for up to 1 week in a sealed container in the fridge, or can be frozen for up to 1 month.

Makes 1 loaf

Gluten-free nut loaf

With its light, fluffy texture, cinnamon kick and unadorned ingredients, this loaf will give you all the energy you need to be inspired. Any number of nut flours or gluten-free flours can be substituted here. For a savoury flavour, replace the stevia with a little Celtic sea salt — let your tastebuds be your guide. This bread is incredibly versatile and can be served up as an accompaniment with avocado, fruit pastes or dips. It will make your heart sing!

150 g (5½ oz/1½ cups) almond meal

30 g (1 oz/¼ cup) walnuts, coarsely chopped

¼ teaspoon gluten-free baking powder

1 teaspoon ground cinnamon

95 g (3¼ oz/¾ cup) arrowroot (tapioca) flour

½ teaspoon sea salt

3 organic eggs

½ teaspoon stevia powder

3 tablespoons grape seed oil

2 tablespoons Homemade Coconut Milk (see page 44)

1 teaspoon apple cider vinegar

Preheat the oven to 180°C (350°F/Gas 4). Grease a 20 x 9 cm (8 x 3½ inch) loaf (bar) tin.

Put the almond meal, walnuts, baking powder, cinnamon, arrowroot flour and salt in a large bowl and mix well with a wooden spoon.

Crack the eggs into a separate bowl and whisk using an electric mixer until pale and fluffy, about 1½ minutes. Add the stevia, grape seed oil, coconut milk and vinegar and mix gently. Pour the mixture into the dry ingredients and stir to combine.

Spoon the mixture into the greased tin and bake for about 40 minutes, or until a skewer inserted in the centre of the loaf comes out clean. Remove the bread from the oven and leave to cool in the tin for a few minutes, before turning out onto a wire rack to cool completely.

Enjoy the bread melt-in-the-mouth warm, or at room temperature with your favourite topping.

Keep in an airtight container in the fridge for up to 6 days, or wrap up tightly and freeze for up to 6 weeks.

Makes 1 loaf

 Health benefits Rich in proteins, healthy fats, omega oils and fibre, nuts are a delicious way to add flavour and crunch to a meal. Walnuts and almonds are densely packed with vitamins B1, B2, B3, B6 and E, and are mineral-rich too, containing manganese, copper, magnesium, phosphorus, iron and zinc. They are reported to lower levels of harmful LDL cholesterol when consumed daily.

Super seeded bread

You can use any combination of seeds for this loaf: fennel, caraway, linseeds (flax seeds), sunflower seeds, sesame seeds, pepitas (pumpkin seeds) or chia seeds.

350 g (12 oz/2¹/₃ cups) gluten-free
   self-raising flour
1¹/₄ cups mixed seeds
¹/₄ teaspoon sea salt
¹/₄ teaspoon stevia powder
4 organic eggs
1 teaspoon apple cider vinegar
3 tablespoons grape seed oil
3 tablespoons Homemade Coconut
   Milk (see page 44)
125 ml (4 fl oz/¹/₂ cup) filtered water
extra sunflower or other seeds,
   for topping

Preheat the oven to 175°C (345°F/Gas 4). Grease and flour a 20 x 9 cm (8 x 3¹/₂ inch) loaf (bar) tin.

In a bowl, combine the flour, mixed seeds, salt and stevia.

In a separate bowl, beat the eggs with an electric mixer until pale and fluffy, about 2 minutes. Stir in the vinegar, grape seed oil, coconut milk and water. Pour the mixture into the dry ingredients and mix well.

Spoon the mixture into the prepared tin, then smooth the surface with the back of a spoon. Scatter some extra seeds over the top.

Bake for 40 minutes, or until a skewer inserted in the centre of the loaf comes out clean. Turn out onto a wire rack to cool.

This bread keeps well for a day or two at room temperature, but should then be kept in the fridge. It can also be wrapped up tightly and frozen for up to 6 weeks.

Makes 1 loaf

basics

Lee's jam jar dressing

This dressing is the perfect accompaniment to any kind of healthy salad or mixed leaves; I love it so much I use it on almost every meal — even drizzled over side vegetables such as green beans, and as a marinade when baking roasts. Splashed over salads and vegetables, the healthy oils and lemon in the dressing help absorb all the food nutrients into your body.

125 ml (4 fl oz/1/2 cup) extra virgin
    olive oil
125 ml (4 fl oz/1/2 cup) grape seed oil
2 tablespoons apple cider vinegar
1 small garlic clove, crushed
2 tablespoons lemon juice

Place all the ingredients in a jar and season well with sea salt and freshly ground black pepper. Screw the lid on tightly and shake! It's as simple as that.

The dressing will keep for up to 5 days in the fridge.

Makes 375 ml (13 fl oz/11/2 cups)

Hollandaise

4 organic egg yolks
1 tablespoon lemon juice
1 tablespoon filtered water
210 ml (71/2 fl oz) grape seed oil,
    warmed (melted organic butter is
    better if you can tolerate it)

Place the egg yolks, lemon juice and water in a blender or mini food processor and blend on low speed for 20–30 seconds.

With the motor running slowly, pour in the oil or melted butter in a thin, steady stream and keep blending until the mixture becomes thick and creamy. If it becomes too thick, add a few drops of warm water.

The hollandaise will keep in a sterile, tightly sealed jar in the fridge for up to 7 days.

Makes about 250 ml (9 fl oz/1 cup)

Mayonnaise

I used to open my refrigerator and wonder why my jumbo jar of mayo was still sitting there as fresh as a daisy after 6 months. It was still alive long after the expiry date, so I nicknamed it George Burns. Whenever I said 'Can you pass me the George Burns?' at the family dinner table, I would be met with quizzical stares, followed by a rolling of the eyes. Well, I'm glad to say that my new-style dairy-free mayo has put a definitive end to all of that. Use it as a condiment, a base dressing for salads or as a dip with crunchy vegetable chips.

1 organic egg
1 tablespoon lemon juice
¼ teaspoon sea salt
185 ml (6 fl oz/¾ cup) grape seed oil
60 ml (2 fl oz/¼ cup) extra virgin olive oil

Crack the egg into a blender or mini food processor and blend on low speed. Add the lemon juice and salt and blend for a few seconds. With the motor still running, very slowly drizzle in the grape seed and olive oils. Keep blending until the mayonnaise is thick and smooth.

The mayo can be stored in the fridge in a sterile, tightly sealed jar for up to 7 days.

Makes about 250 ml (9 fl oz/1 cup)

Aïoli

My friend Juliet, who has a penchant for naming things, loves to call this 'alloy'. We giggle with delight whenever we are out in a café and she asks the waiter for some alloy on the side. This alloy can be locked up — I mean knocked up — in just moments, and works well as a dip or a dressing on salads and burgers.

2 organic egg yolks
4 large garlic cloves, crushed
1 tablespoon lemon juice
1 tablespoon filtered water
310 ml (10¾ fl oz/1¼ cups) grape seed oil

Beat the egg yolks and garlic in a bowl with a wooden spoon. Now add the lemon juice and water and keep stirring. Slowly add the grape seed oil, stirring continually until the desired consistency is reached. Add more lemon juice and sea salt to taste if needed.

The 'alloy' will keep in the fridge in a sterile, tightly sealed jar for up to 7 days.

Makes about 350 ml (12 fl oz)

Caesar dressing

Authentic in flavour and taste, this is one of the quickest, easiest recipes I can think of — and knowing that it's super healthy is an added reason to whip up a batch of this thick, creamy and wickedly good dressing. It's not just limited to Caesar salads — try plonking it on gluten-free pizza bases or use it as a marinade for chicken.

1 organic egg
3 tablespoons grape seed oil
3 anchovies, finely chopped
1 tablespoon lemon juice
1 teaspoon finely grated lemon zest
1 teaspoon apple cider vinegar
3 garlic cloves, roughly chopped

Place all the ingredients in a mini food processor or blender and whiz until smooth.

The dressing can be stored in the fridge in a sterile, tightly sealed jar for up to 7 days.

Makes about 250 ml (9 fl oz/1 cup)

Chicken spice rub

Meats taste a thousand times better when seasoned with simple spice rubs before cooking. Rubs add bursts of flavour and texture, especially when barbecuing and grilling (broiled). Homemade rubs are super easy to bring together — and you'll save money too, as you won't be paying extra for yukky additives in colourful packaging. Experiment with this basic rub recipe by adding your own herbs and spices. Use the freshest spices for best results.

2 tablespoons white peppercorns
1 tablespoon black peppercorns
120 g (4¼ oz/1 cup) fennel seeds
3 tablespoons coriander (cilantro) seeds
2 tablespoons ground cumin
1 tablespoon dried sage
1 teaspoon dried basil
2 tablespoons sea salt

Place a dry, heavy-based frying pan over medium heat. Add the white and black peppercorns, fennel seeds and coriander seeds and toast until aromatic and lightly browned. Spread them out on a plate and leave to cool.

Transfer the mixture to a blender or mini food processor and add the cumin, sage, basil and salt. Blend until the mixture resembles a fine powder.

The spice rub can be stored in a tightly sealed jar in a cool spot in your pantry for up to 2 months.

Makes about 1¼ cups

Homemade tomato sauce

I love tomatoes. There are so many reasons to splurge on this wonderful, voluptuous food. Whether it's a fruit or a vegetable is irrelevant — just pass me the sea salt and cracked pepper. Surprisingly uncomplicated, this sauce can be used as a foundation for bolognaise, stroked upon a gluten-free pizza base or plopped over scrambled eggs. Extended simmering will thicken up the sauce and give it a more intense and robust appeal, melding the flavours together. It will stop you in your tracks.

2 tablespoons extra virgin olive oil

1 red capsicum (pepper), very finely chopped

2 garlic cloves, crushed

1 onion, chopped

1 kg (2 lb 4 oz) tomatoes, skinned and chopped (see tip below)

3 tablespoons sugar-free tomato paste (concentrated purée)

6 drops liquid stevia

1/2 teaspoon sea salt

1 tablespoon chopped mixed basil and parsley

Heat the olive oil in a deep, heavy-based frying pan. Add the capsicum, garlic and onion and cook over medium heat, stirring often, until the onion is translucent, about 6–8 minutes.

Add the tomatoes, tomato paste, stevia, salt and a few grinds of black pepper. Bring to the boil, then reduce the heat, cover and simmer for about 20 minutes, or until the sauce is thick.

Stir in the basil and parsley and taste for salt and pepper, adjusting if necessary. Remove from the heat and leave to cool.

You can now strain the sauce through a sieve if you prefer a smooth tomato passata (puréed tomato) sauce. This will yield about 250 ml (9 fl oz/1 cup).

The tomato sauce will keep in the fridge in a sterile, tightly sealed jar for up to a week. It can also be frozen for up to a month in small containers, to thaw as needed.

Makes 500 ml (17 fl oz/2 cups)

 Supercharged tip Here's how to skin tomatoes... Flick the kettle on and place tomatoes in a medium-sized bowl. Using a sharp knife, carefully make a slit down one side of each tomato. Once the kettle has boiled, pour the boiling water over them, ensuring they are all covered, then let them relax in the water for a few minutes. You'll notice that the skins will start to peel off. Strain the water from the bowl and allow the tomatoes to cool. You'll now find it super easy to skin them.

Nutty dipping sauce

This sauce is as simple as sauté, stir and serve. It can be served as a dipping sauce or salad dressing, as well as a no-nasties satay sauce over chicken skewers.

1 teaspoon sesame oil
1 onion, finely chopped
2 garlic cloves, crushed
1/2 teaspoon grated fresh ginger
1 small red chilli, seeded and
   finely chopped
270 ml (91/2 fl oz) tin coconut milk
   (no additives)
125 g (41/2 oz/1/2 cup) almond butter
1 tablespoon wheat-free tamari
6 drops liquid stevia

Heat the sesame oil in a frying pan over medium heat. Add the onion, garlic, ginger and chilli and sauté until the onion becomes translucent, about 5 minutes.

Stir in the remaining ingredients and simmer for another 5 minutes.

Transfer to a serving dish and serve.

The sauce will keep in the fridge in a sterile, tightly sealed jar for up to 5 days; it also freezes well.

Makes 375 ml (13 fl oz/11/2) cups

Sweet yellow squash sauce

When life hands you squash, use them to make sweet sauciness. If I'm ever craving apple sauce, sweet yellow squash always satisfies with its delicate and subtle flavour. It's an appealing alternative to conventional highly processed apple sauce, with a much lower fructose level. Serve this sauce with roast pork, or alongside your favourite grilled (broiled) or barbecued meats.

130 g (41/2 oz/1 cup) diced yellow button
   (pattypan) squash
1 tablespoon grape seed oil, or organic
   butter if tolerated (optional)
1 teaspoon lemon juice
liquid stevia, to taste

Steam the squash until just tender. Transfer to a blender or food processor and add the grape seed oil, lemon juice and a pinch of sea salt. Blend until smooth, then add a drop or two of stevia, to taste.

Spoon the sauce into a serving bowl, or into a covered container if not using it straight away. It will keep in the fridge for 2 days.

Makes 250 ml (9 fl oz/1 cup)

Homemade chicken stock

On Sundays I like to make my own full-flavoured stock, with some of the leftover in-season vegies in the fridge and a whole chicken. I let the stock simmer on the back burner while everything else is happening. Once you've made your own stock you'll never go back to the commercial varieties again — and you'll be able to sniff out an additive-filled stock cube from ten paces. Real stock tastes so much richer and enhances everything. And it's incredibly easy to make.

1.6 kg (3 lb 8 oz) organic chicken
2 litres (70 fl oz/8 cups) filtered water
2 tablespoons lemon juice
1 large onion, chopped
3 celery stalks, chopped
2 garlic cloves
1 bunch (100 g/3½ oz) parsley
1 bunch (20 g/¾ oz) rosemary
1 bunch (20 g/¾ oz) thyme
2 bay leaves

Place the chicken in a stockpot with the rest of the ingredients and add a few grinds of black pepper. Bring to a simmer, skimming off any scum that rises to the surface. Reduce the heat to low and simmer for 2–3 hours, adding extra water now and then if needed to keep the chicken covered.

Carefully remove the chicken from the stock (it may break up) and leave to cool. Strain the stock into a large bowl and refrigerate. The fat will rise to the top and congeal, making it easy to lift off and discard.

The stock will keep in a covered container in the fridge for up to 2 weeks. It can also be frozen in airtight containers for up to 3 months.

The chicken meat can be removed from the carcass and used in soups, salads or sandwiches.

Makes about 2 litres (70 fl oz/8 cups)

Vanilla custard

This recipe contains dairy in the form of butter. Some people with lactose and casein intolerances can still enjoy butter, but if you have trouble with butter, you can still enjoy the Coconut Whipped Cream and Cashew Nut Cream recipes opposite.

185 ml (6 fl oz/3/4 cup) filtered water
3 teaspoons powdered gelatine
3 organic eggs
8 drops liquid stevia
125 g (4 1/2 oz) unsalted organic butter,
   softened
1 1/2 teaspoons natural vanilla extract

Pour the water into a small saucepan and sprinkle the gelatine on top. Leave to sit for about a minute, or until the gelatine softens. Place the mixture over medium heat and stir constantly with a wooden spoon for 3 minutes.

Spoon the contents into a blender. Add the eggs, stevia, butter and vanilla, then blend on low speed until the custard turns pale, about 2 minutes.

Spoon the custard into a covered container and chill in the fridge. Stir before using.

The custard will keep in the fridge for 3 days.

Makes 375 ml (13 fl oz/1 1/2 cups)

Coconut whipped cream

For this recipe to work you must use a coconut milk that contains no stabilisers (such as soy lecithin or guar gum), which can cause problems for people who are gluten intolerant, so check the label before selecting a brand.

2 x 400 ml (14 fl oz) tins full-fat coconut milk (no additives), **chilled overnight**
1 teaspoon stevia powder
1/2 teaspoon lemon juice
1 tablespoon natural vanilla extract
3 tablespoons coconut flour

Without shaking the tins of coconut milk, remove the lids. Carefully spoon off the cream that has separated and settled on the surface of the milk and place in a chilled bowl — you will get about 6 tablespoons from each tin. Reserve the remaining coconut milk for other recipes.

Using electric beaters, whip the coconut cream until a little thickened. Whisk in the stevia, lemon juice and vanilla. Gradually add the coconut flour, beating it in a bit at a time, until the cream has thickened.

Spoon into a covered container and refrigerate for 2 hours before serving. The cream keeps well in the refrigerator for up to 3 days.

Makes about 2 cups

Cashew nut cream

Spread this luscious stuff on toast, spoon it onto pancakes or dollop over your favourite seasonal fruit.

250 g (9 oz/1 cup) cashew nut butter or
    155 g (5½ oz/1 cup) raw cashew nuts
170 ml (5½ fl oz/2/3 cup) filtered water
8 drops liquid stevia
1½ teaspoons natural vanilla extract

Place all the ingredients in a food processor and whiz until smooth and creamy. If using cashew nuts, you may need to add a little more water and process until smooth.

The cream can be stored in the fridge in a covered container for up to 1 week.

Makes about 1½ cups

index

acknowledgements

I would like to extend a huge thank you to Murdoch Books, in particular Kylie Walker, Juliet Rogers, the amazing Gabriella Sterio, Jo Glynn, super chef Grace Campbell, Katia Nizic, and editor extraordinaire Katri Hilden, for your enthusiasm and belief in this book. Thank you to Steve Brown who did a wonderful job creating gorgeous photos, and the super stylist Marie Helene Clauzon—I adore your style.

Thank you to my friends and colleagues who have been so generous with their time and advice; Quentin McDermott, Grahame Grassby, Rena Monemvasitis, Louise Cornege, Hayley Dutton, Juliet Potter, Dan Toomey, Monique Richards, Olivia Richardson, Julia Gauci and Cindy Sciberras for the freshly laid eggs and recipe feedback.

Thank you to my dynamo illustrator, Caroline Thaw, www.carolinethaw.net, who created all the beautiful imagery on my website, www.superchargedfood.com. Justin S, I appreciate your creative input and the fact you like fonts just as much as I do.

Masterchefs Emma and Lucinda, your cooking tips and advice have been invaluable. A massive thank you to the extraordinary Alex von Kotze, the "roxinater" Roxy and to Arizona, Carol, Lorraine, Clive and Ben for your love and support. Sebastian, a big appreciative thank you for your unyielding patience and for happily taste-testing everything from spinach bread to raw zucchini pasta (zoodles).

And thanks to my talented and beautiful daughter, Tamsin. When your school friends said the sea-salt and activated ACV almonds were the best snacks they'd ever tasted, it was music to my ears! You are the best daughter in the world. I love you.

Published in 2012 by Murdoch Books, an imprint of Allen & Unwin.

Murdoch Books Australia
83 Alexander Street
Crows Nest NSW 2065
Phone: +61 (0) 2 8425 0100
Fax: +61 (0) 2 9906 2218
www.murdochbooks.com.au
info@murdochbooks.com.au

Murdoch Books UK
Erico House, 6th Floor
93–99 Upper Richmond Road
Putney, London SW15 2TG
Phone: +44 (0) 20 8785 5995
www.murdochbooks.co.uk
info@murdochbooks.co.uk

For Corporate Orders & Custom Publishing contact Noel Hammond,
National Business Development Manager, Murdoch Books Australia

Publisher: Kylie Walker
Designer: Alex Frampton
Photographer: Steve Brown
Stylist: Marie Helene Clauzon
Project editor: Gabriella Sterio
Editor: Katri Hilden

A cataloguing-in-publication entry is available from the catalogue of the National
Library of Australia at www.nla.gov.au.

A catalogue record for this book is available from the British Library.

Colour reproduction by Splitting Image, Clayton, Victoria.

Printed by Hang Tai Printing Company Limited, China.
Reprinted in 2012, 2013, 2014

IMPORTANT: Those who might be at risk from the effects of salmonella poisoning
(the elderly, pregnant women, young children and those suffering from immune
deficiency diseases) should consult their doctor with any concerns about eating
raw eggs.

OVEN GUIDE: You may find cooking times vary depending on the oven you are
using. For fan-forced ovens, as a general rule, set the oven temperature 20°C (35°F)
lower than indicated in the recipe.

MEASURES GUIDE: We have used 20 ml (4 teaspoon) tablespoon measures.
If you are using a 15 ml (3 teaspoon) tablespoon add an extra teaspoon of the
ingredient for each tablespoon specified.